S0-HJG-173

Aernout Mik

Reversal Room

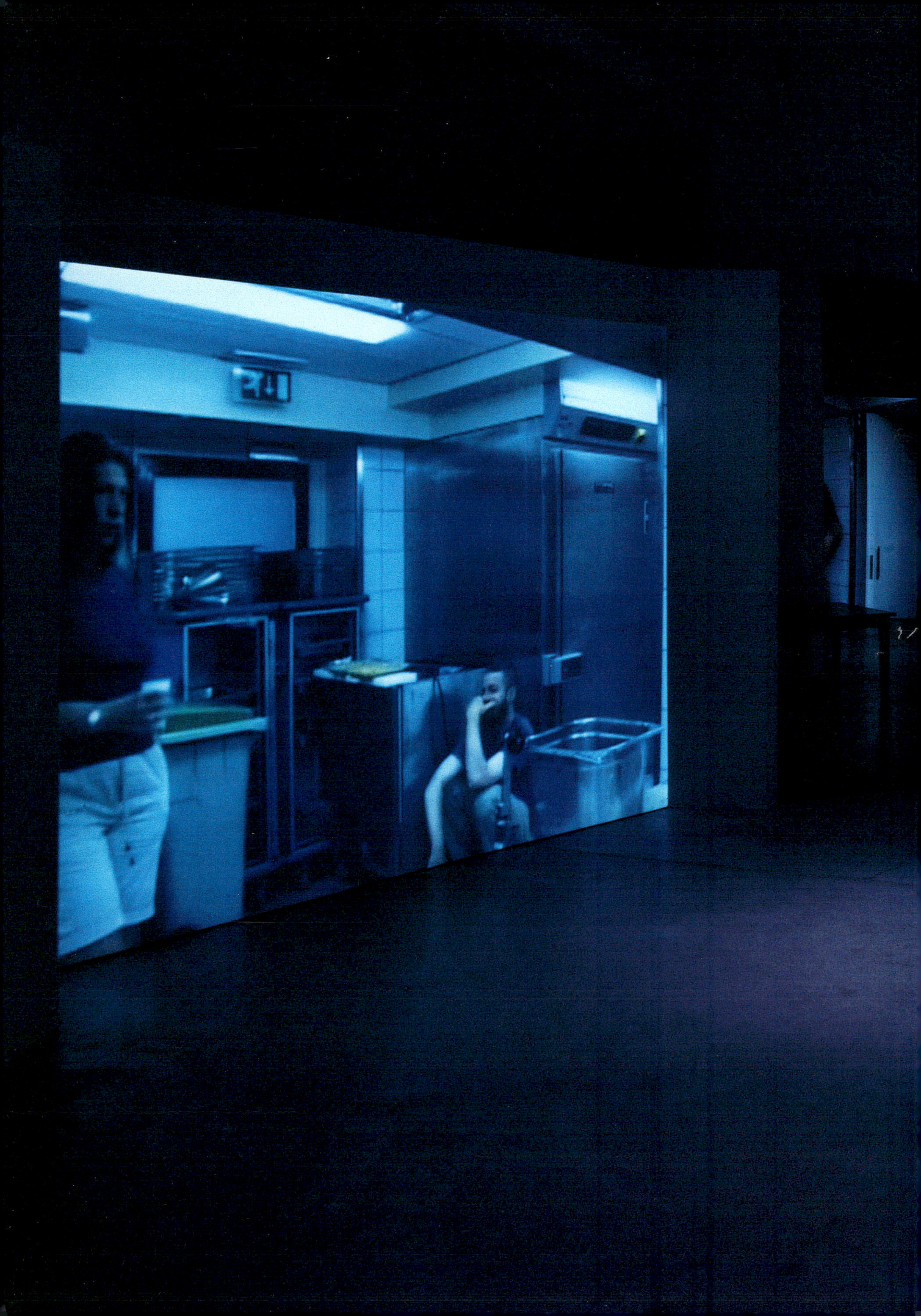

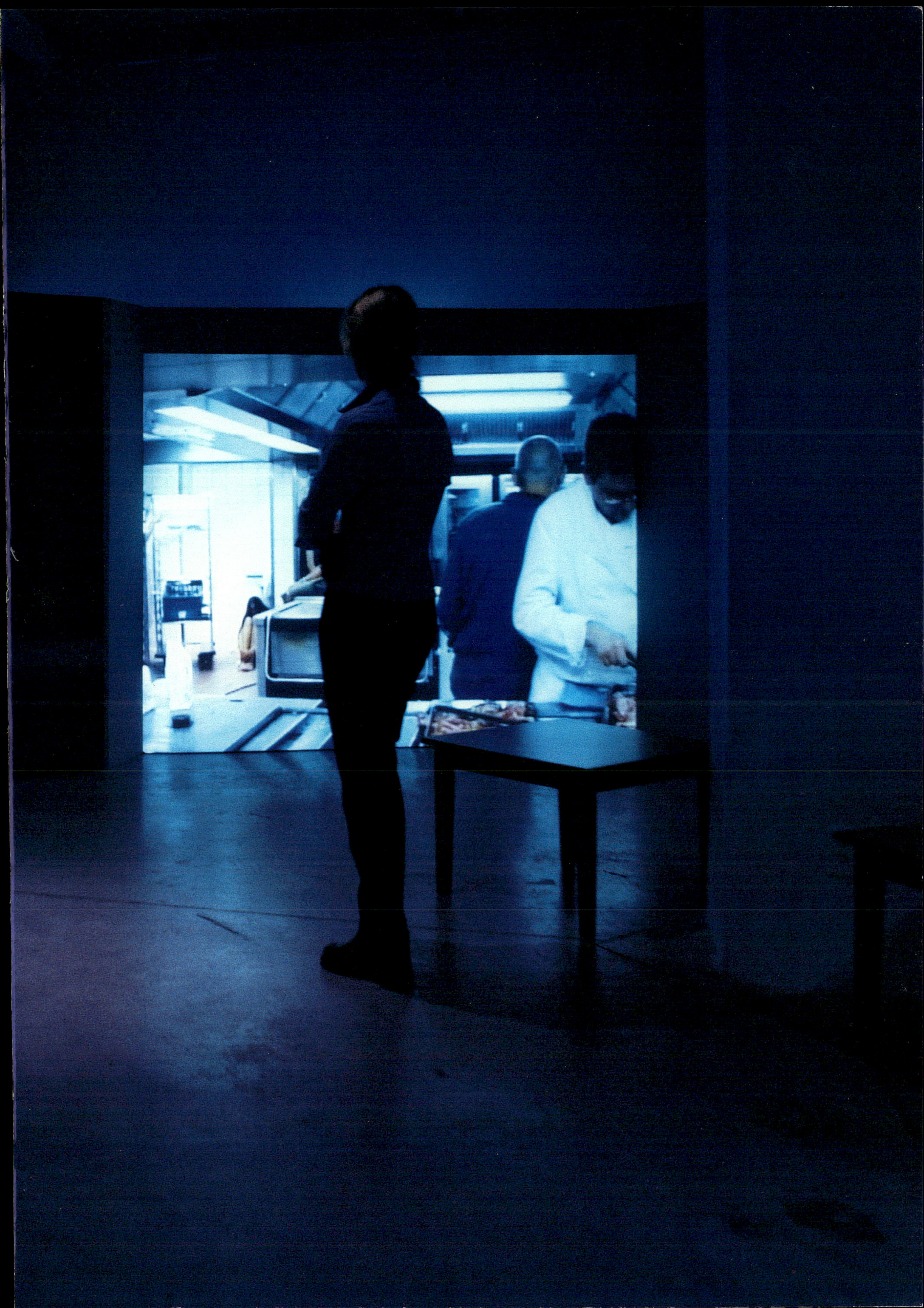

Aernout Mik

Reversal Room

Philip Monk

The Power Plant

22 September – 18 November 2001

© 2002 by The Power Plant
Contemporary Art Gallery at Harbourfront Centre
231 Queens Quay West, Toronto, Ontario, Canada M5J 2G8
(416) 973-4949
www.thepowerplant.org

National Library of Canada Cataloguing in Publication Data

Monk, Philip, 1950–
Aernout Mik: Reversal Room

Catalogue of an exhibition held at the Power Plant Contemporary Art Gallery at Harbourfront Centre, Sept. 22–Nov. 18, 2001.

ISBN 0-921047-99-1

1. Mik, Aernout – Exhibitions. I. Mik, Aernout II. Power Plant Contemporary Art Gallery at Harbourfront Centre III. Title.

N6953.M55A4 2002 709'.2 C2002-900285-0

The catalogue and exhibition are made possible with support from the Mondriaan Foundation, Amsterdam and the Royal Netherlands Embassy, Ottawa. Thanks also to the Netherlands Foundation for Visual Arts, Design and Architecture and the Dutch Film Fund for their contributions to the production of *Reversal Room*.

Mondriaan Stichting
(Mondriaan Foundation)

JE MAINTIENDRAI

The Power Plant
Contemporary Art Gallery
Harbourfront centre

Contents

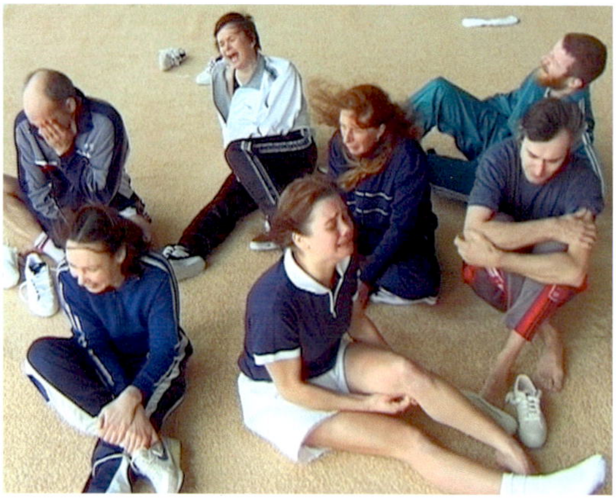

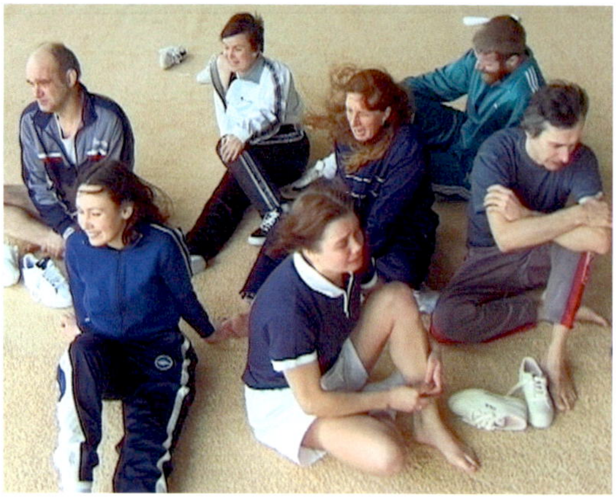

3 laughing and 4 crying, 1998
video installation

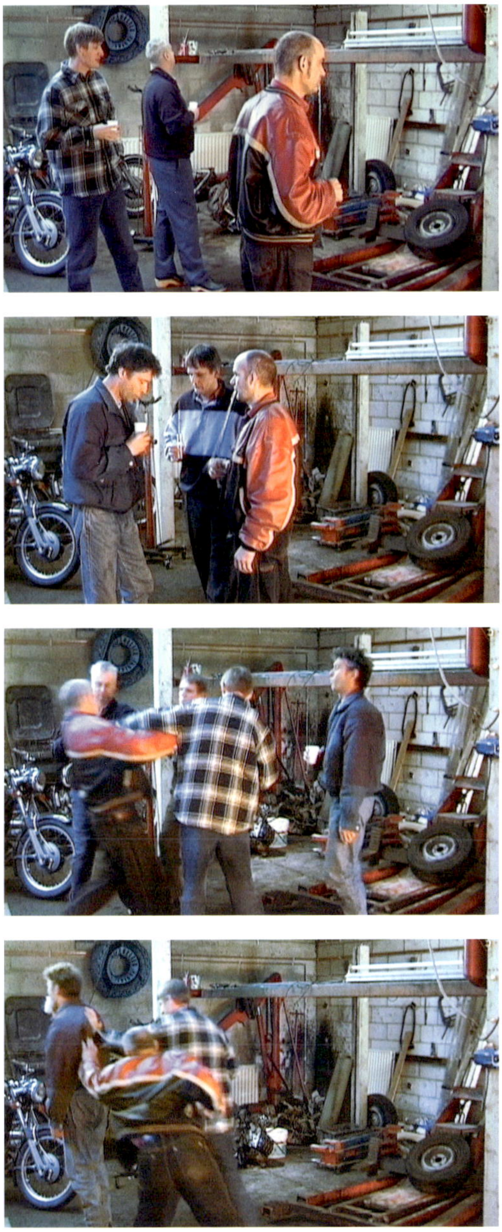

Garage, 1998
video installation

Abode where lost bodies roam each searching for its lost one. Vast enough for search to be in vain. Narrow enough for flight to be in vain. Inside a flattened cylinder fifty metres round and eighteen high for the sake of harmony. The light. Its dimness. Its yellowness. Its omnipresence as though every separate square centimetre were agleam of the some eighty thousand of total surface. Its restlessness at long intervals suddenly stilled like panting at the last. Then all go dead still. It is perhaps the end of their abode. A few seconds and all begins again....

— **Samuel Beckett**, *The Lost Ones*

Almost Normal: The Video Installations of Aernout Mik

Introduction

In Tarkovsky's 1972 science fiction film *Solaris*, an orbiting Soviet space expedition is studying a planet thought to be a giant brain. To the distress of the crew, the planet has the power to generate life-like simulacra of people left behind, created from the memories and desires of the Soviet observers. Yet it can't get everything right: these "monstrous" humanoids do not know quite how to behave entirely like real people. Similarly, the planet can create uncanny images for its visitors. For instance, we witness the protagonist's vision of his father in his home on earth, except it is raining inside the house.

Back on earth, in Aernout Mik's video installations, the images and actions are not quite right either—intentionally so. Sometimes it rains destruction on protagonists who go about their strange business, as in *Softer Catwalk in Collapsing Rooms* (1999), where oblivious figures "sleepwalk" through a collapsing apartment. At other times, his actors evince no proper human response; they pay no attention to each other even though together they engage in extremes of emotion. In *3 laughing and 4 crying* (1998), the two groups performing the actions described by the title are locked in their own solipsistic emotional exercises.

In these and other Mik videos, an identifiable intention seems lacking in an individual's behaviour, while the group seems to follow no recognizable codes of conduct. For instance, in *Garage* (1998) three men mill about in a car mechanic's garage. We are familiar with men socializing in spaces where they feel comfortable, but here the men spew their drinks back into their cups or dribble the liquid down their jackets as they walk backwards. A fourth man enters, but he is immediately pushed off-screen by the other three in some territorial ritual. This action repeats, but with different combinations of men entering and leaving so there is no predictability as to who is assaulted by whom. Having neither a start nor a finish, the unmodulated activity has a pattern but no obvious rationale.

Nothing is ordinary in a Mik video installation; yet nothing, at the same time, is extraordinary. That is, no action rises above the continuity of activity as an isolable event. As viewers, we are able somehow to accommodate ourselves to these odd though unexceptional actions over time precisely because of their continuance, whether we can attribute a meaning to them or not. If we cannot cleave an intention to the protagonists' behaviour, nevertheless, we are part of the flow of their activity, parallel to it — we too participate in Mik's fabrication, temporally captured by its scene.

Describing the behaviour in Mik's videos challenges our language. For instance, "protagonist" should appear in quotation marks because no one's actions are more important than another's. No one stands out as a lead figure as the word implies. And perhaps any mention of our participation should appear bracketed because we do not yet know how our actions are guided by the artificiality of what is immediately given. We do not know what to focus on — the images or the environments Mik constructs around them. Although we are familiar with the codes of the moving image in television and the movies, in video installations these codes are often skewed. But even within Mik's images, the activity is puzzling: real yet artificial, documentary yet fictive, they operate on two levels simultaneously.

The cameras catch something real, but the activity is evidently directed. Mik gives instructions to his non-professional actors and extras, but allows no rehearsal. Indeed, Mik's works have the feel of a film shoot, where actions are scripted within the close confines of the set and recorded within the strict framing and movement of the camera. And this, in fact, is the way his works are produced — although as one extended scene without editing. (There is the occasional cut in Mik's video but it does not alter the general flow of activity.) Here the affinity to traditional narrative film ends: in Mik's works there is no acting, motivation, or story, nor is there a development, climax, or conclusion.

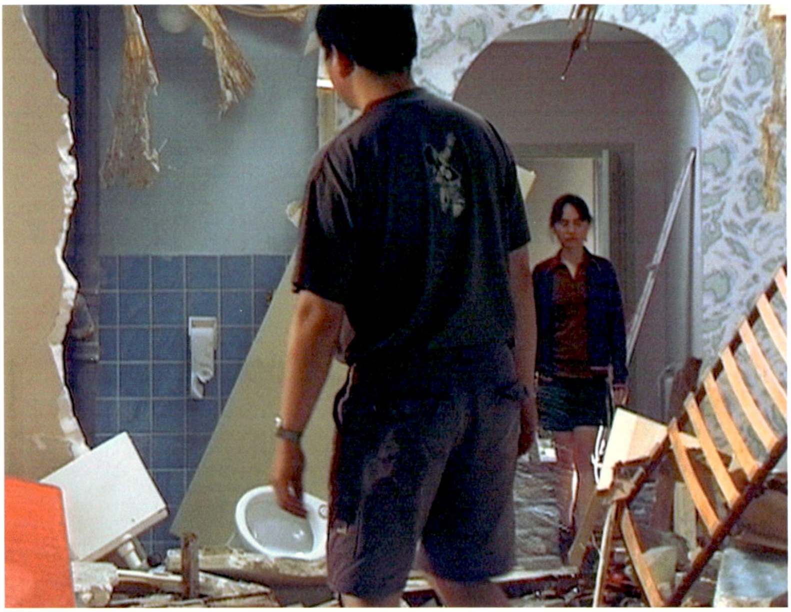

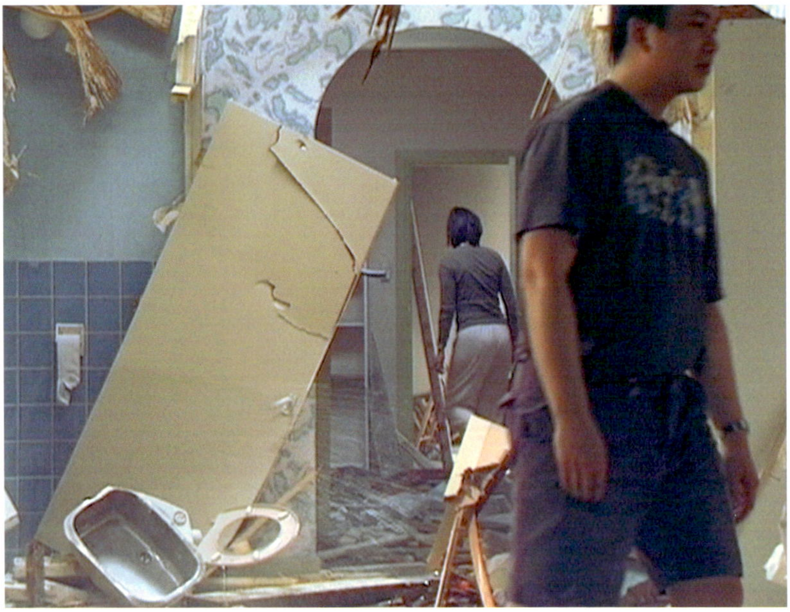

Softer Catwalk in Collapsing Rooms, 1999

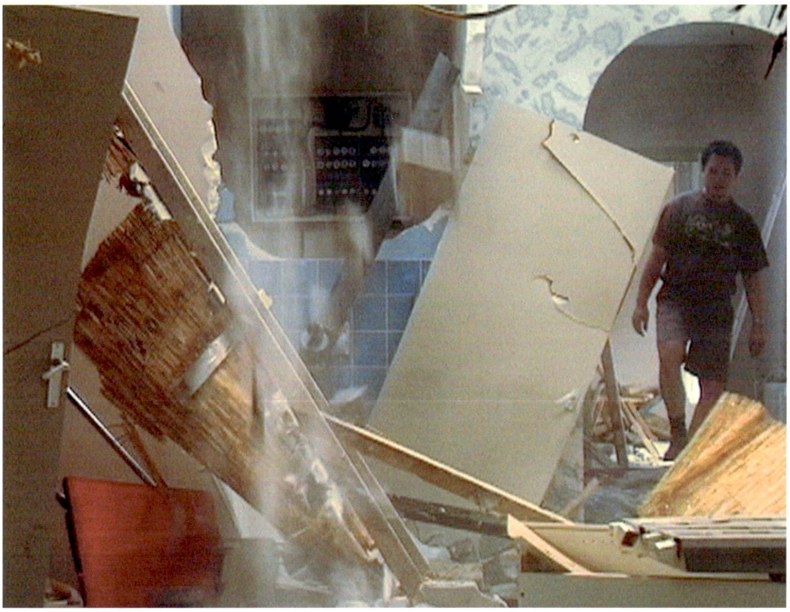

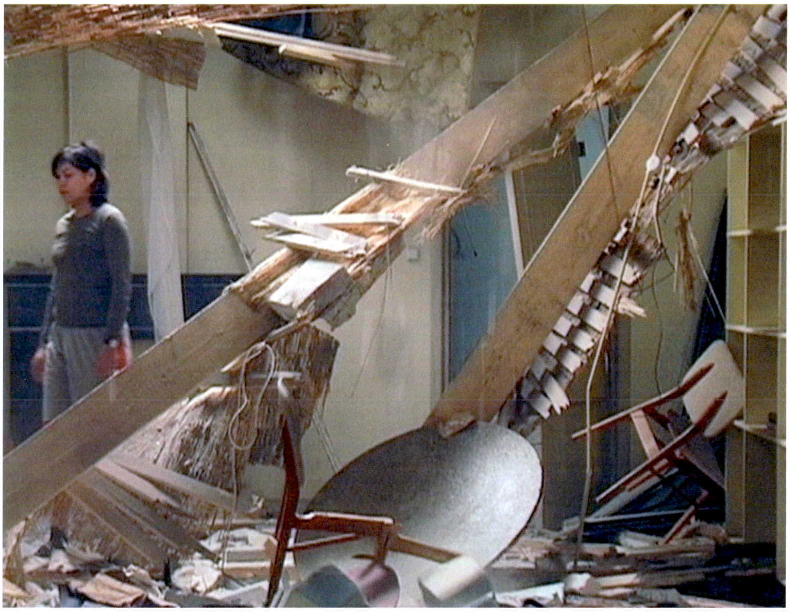

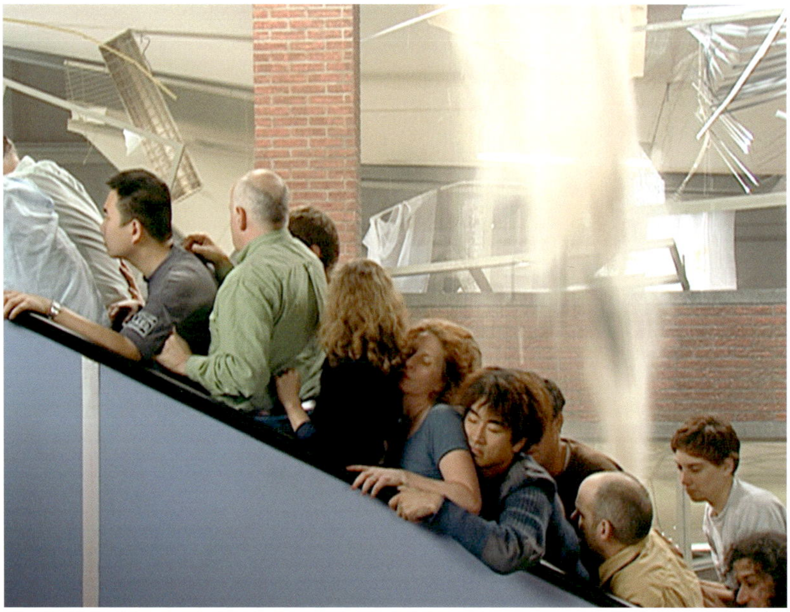

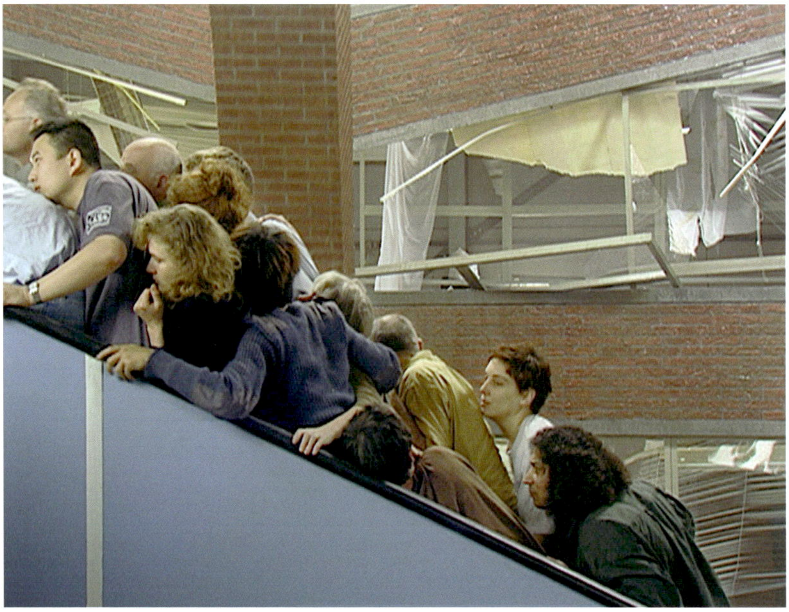

Organic Escalator, 2000

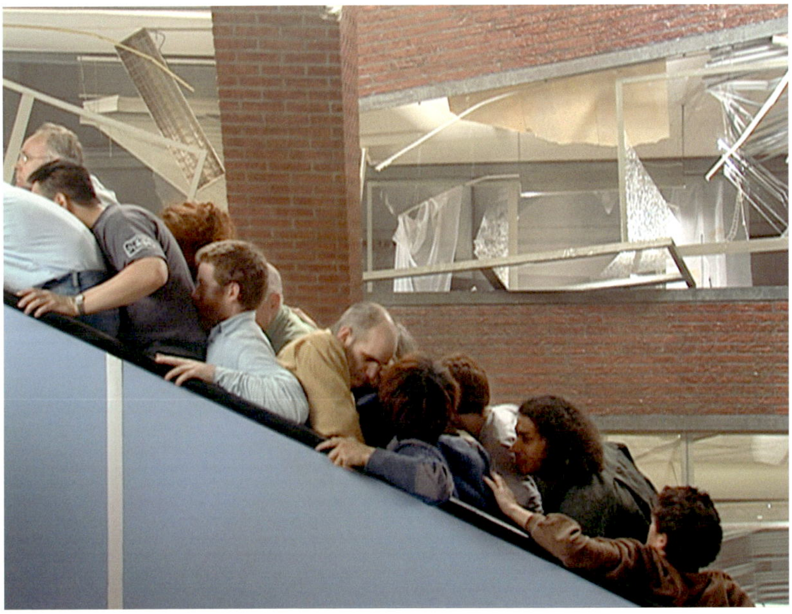

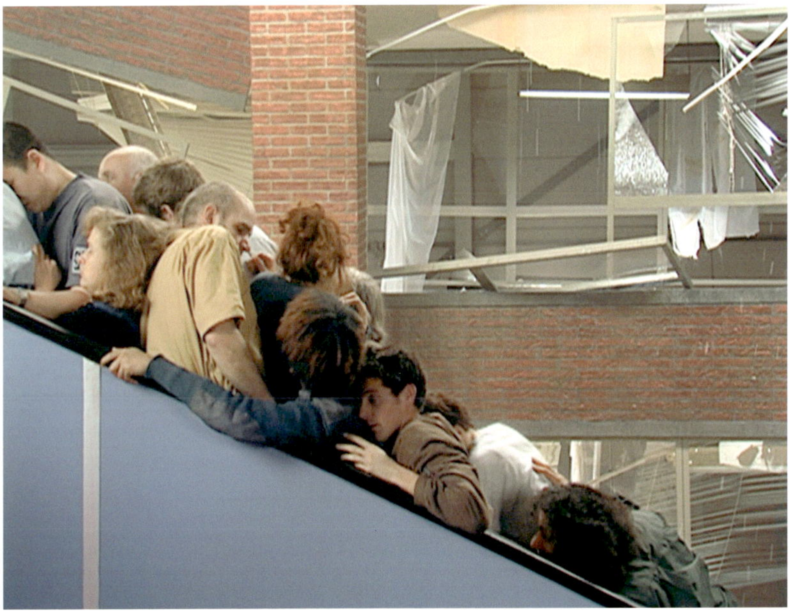

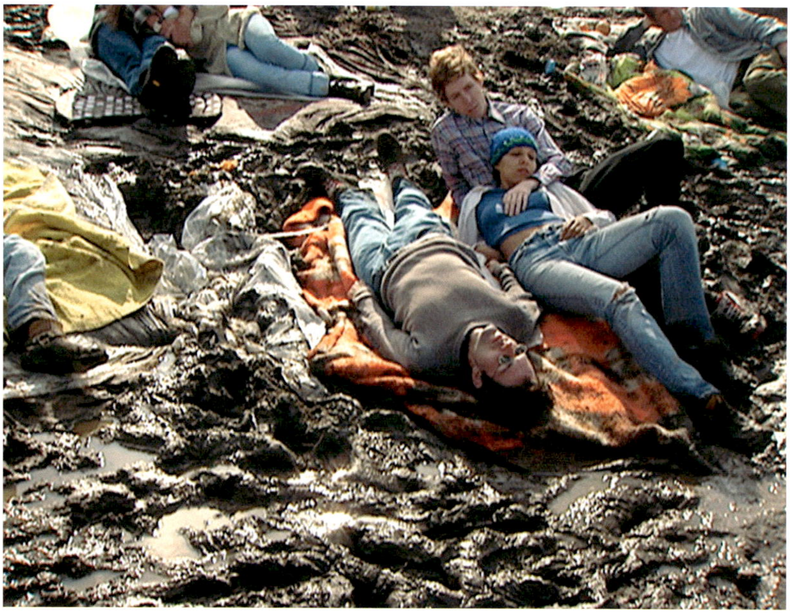

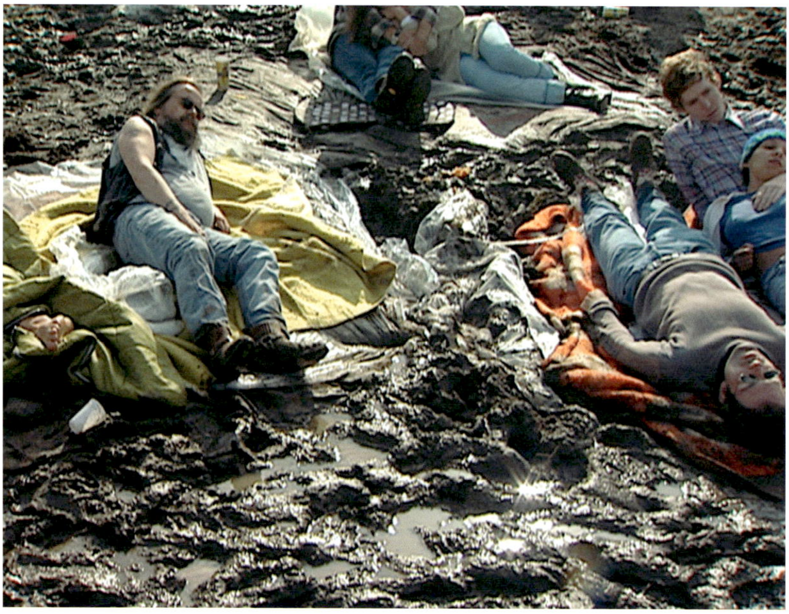

Lumber, 2000

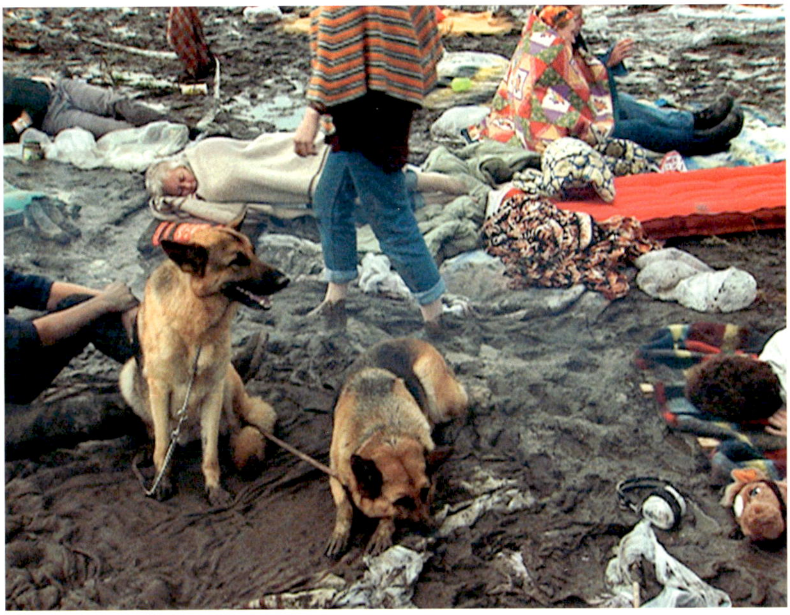

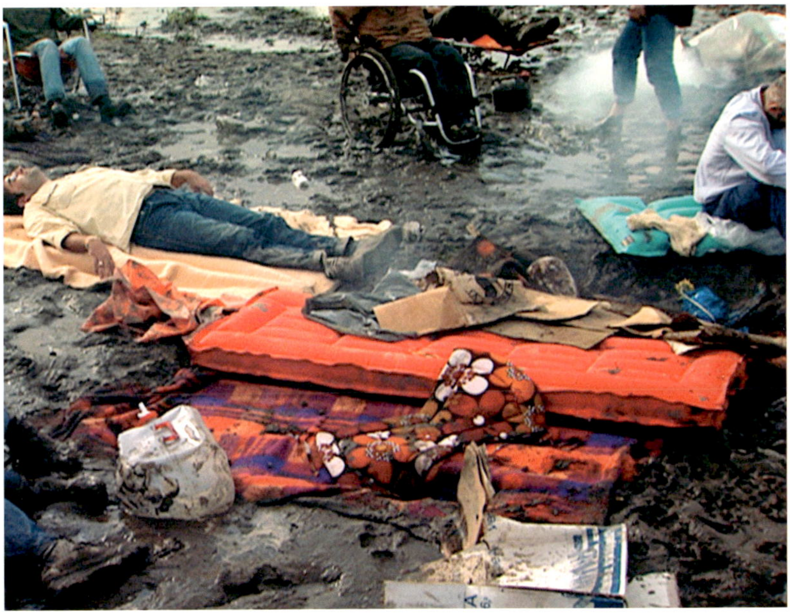

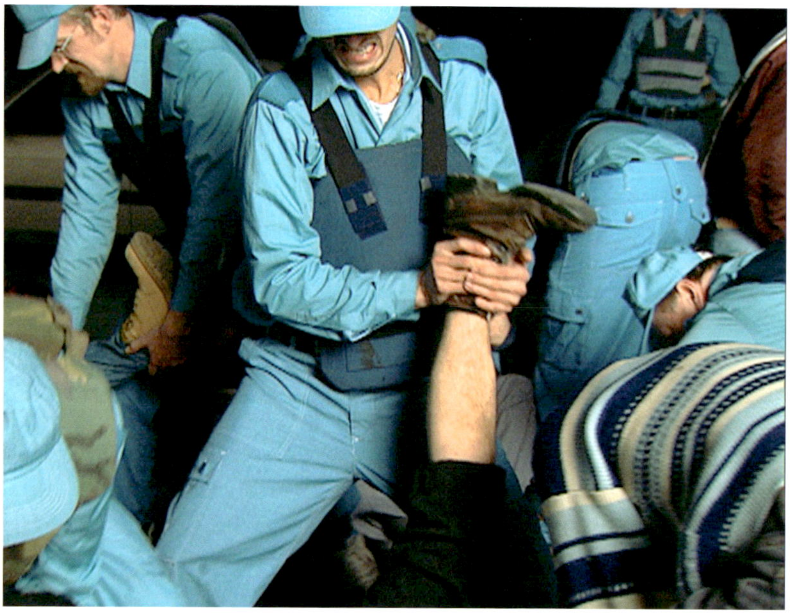

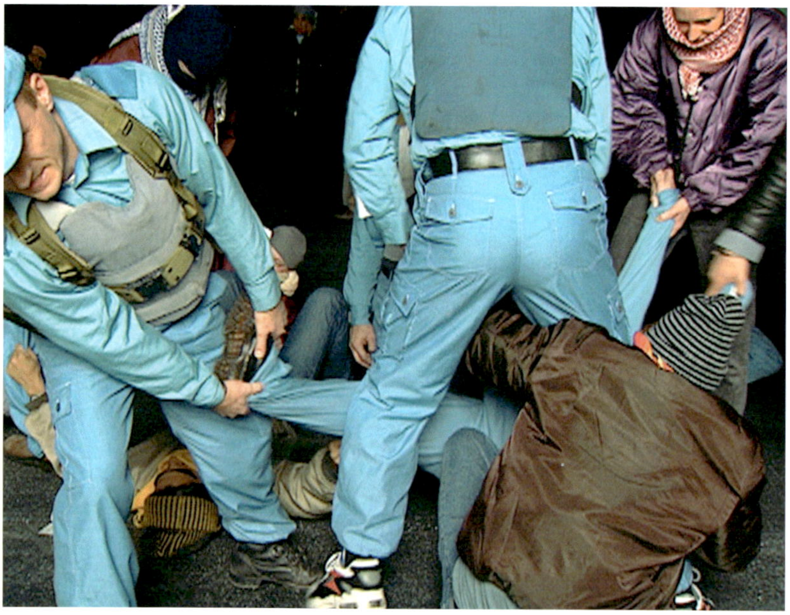

Glutinosity, 2001

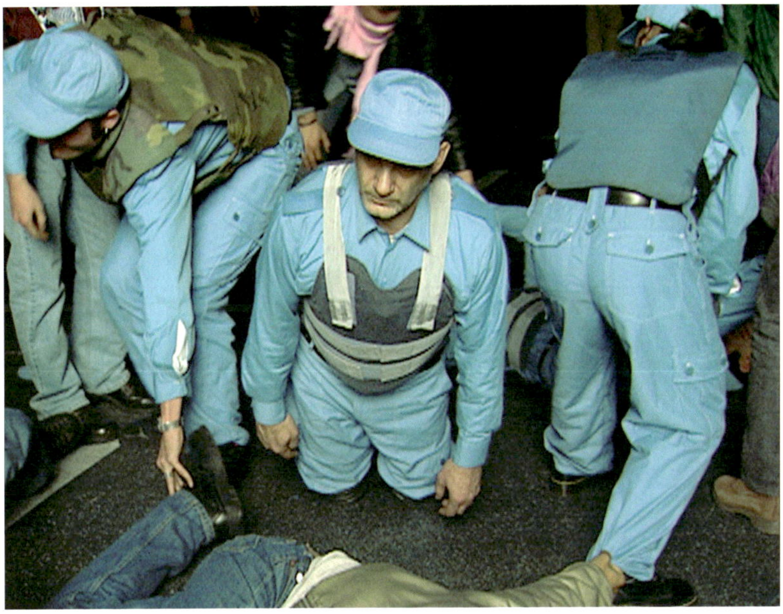

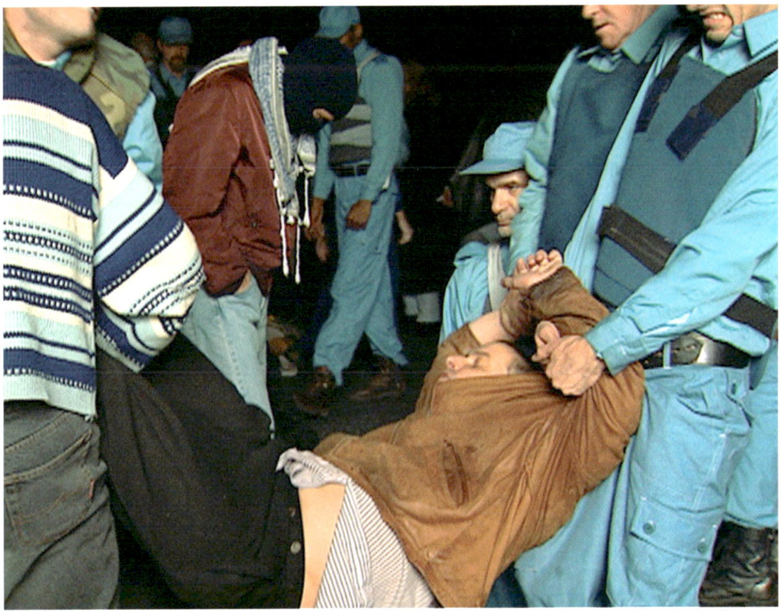

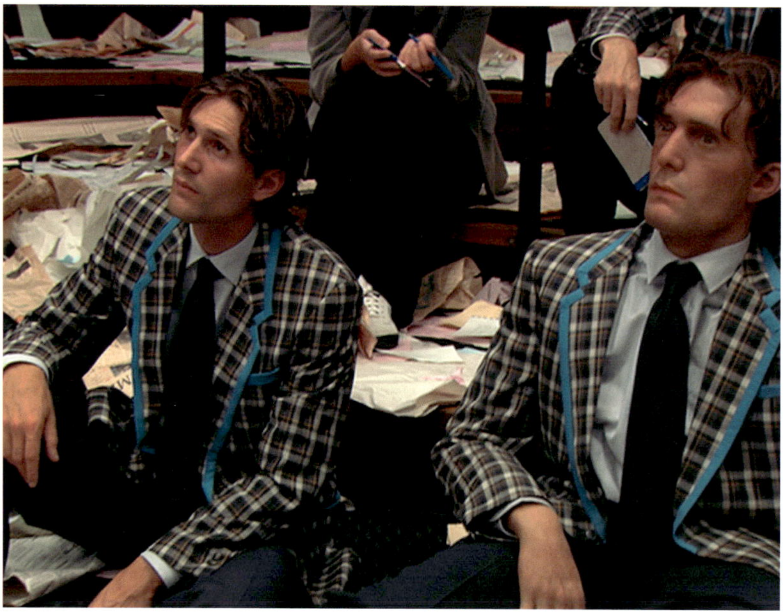

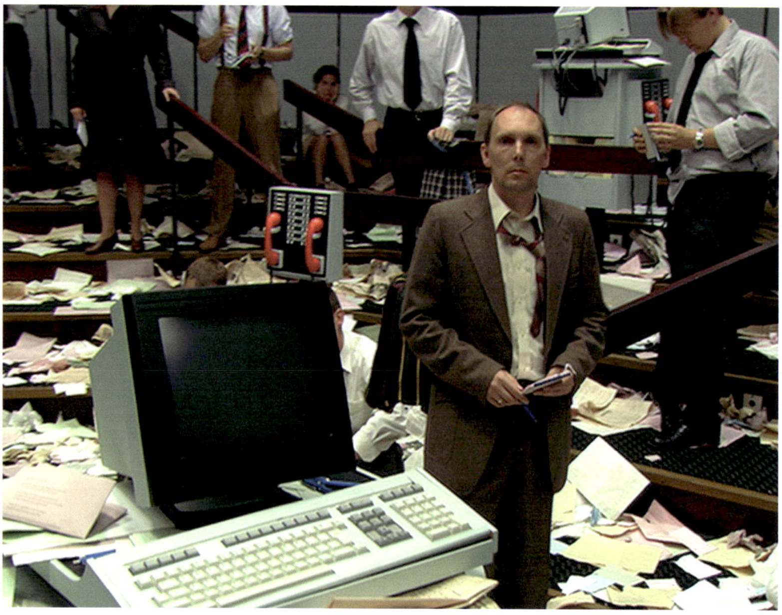

Middlemen, 2001

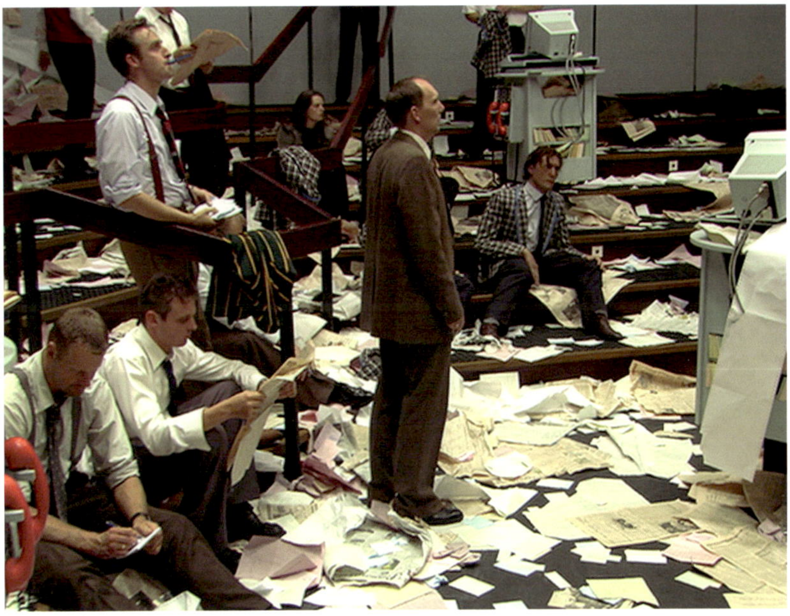

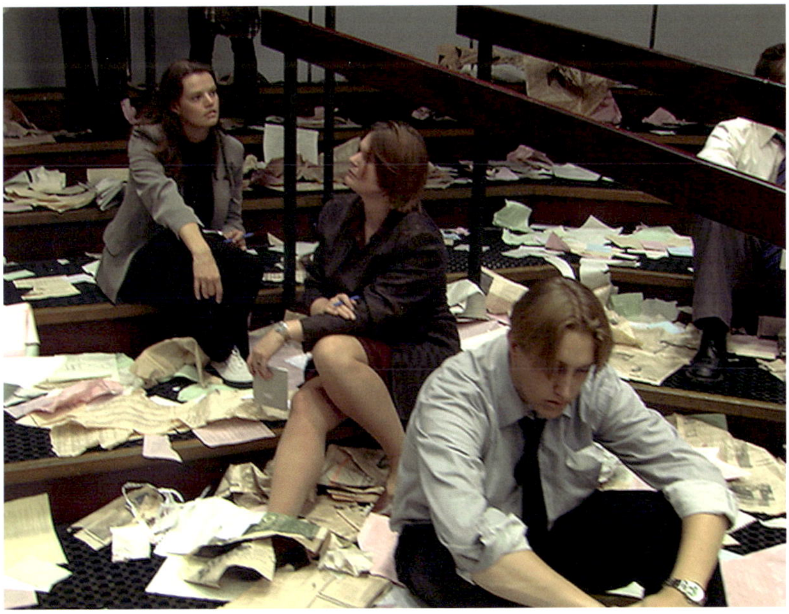

Languages of Action

> I don't mean to dismiss self-awareness altogether, just the part of it that promotes the idea of an individual as an independent creation who can be looked at as separate from his environment and other people and objects in space. You're always someone else than you think you are. You're always saying something different than you think you are saying. What your whole body has to say is so much more complex.
> — **Aernout Mik**

Unless physically threatened or surprised, we hardly ever respond consciously to our immediate surroundings, but navigate them routinely. While walking or driving, our attention is usually only half there: at the same time, we might be absent-mindedly rehearsing a previous conversation or anticipating a future meeting. Even though we might be physically in the present, we are seldom mentally there. Mental chatter doesn't affect activity, though; our bodies are habitually in control. However, when we describe our behaviour, the relation of language to action differs; our conduct takes on an intention it might not have originally possessed. The language of agency, with its presiding ego, is embedded in our speech. The subject-object nature of our language makes it action oriented and predominately narrative in character.

In the mid-twentieth century, behavioural scientists such as Ray Birdwhistle attempted to articulate another language for describing behaviour more attuned to the signals the body sends. They conceived of the body itself as integral to social communication. Gestural components of this other "language" were isolated from verbal utterances and studied for their significance. In a branch of behavioural science research called kinesics, film cameras and slow motion recorders were used. This controlled situation is perhaps akin to the contemporary analyses of group behaviour we find in Mik's video installations.

There is none of the transparency demanded by scientific objectivity to Mik's methods, though. The artist controls the context (having constructed it) and the situation (having dictated the activity), so that we cannot examine the idiosyncratic behaviour apart from the conditions that form it. Further, he contaminates the space of observation — that of the video — by letting it bleed into our own. Moreover, we are not given criteria for observation, or even a defined object of study. What would we isolate as significant in the behaviour when social rules seem suspended? There are no evident rules for either performing or reading behaviour.

Mik's videos appear to examine routine behaviour. But what seems normal to us is obviously different to his participants. Intentionality, our guide for judging the behaviour of others, is curiously absent. Exterior action has been sundered from interior motivation; a void seems to exist between intention and action, between will and its fulfillment. Behaviour is determined no more by inner motivation than by outer context. Mik's participants do not respond conventionally or rationally to the demands or threats of their milieu. Nonetheless, they persist in their actions. Obviously other criteria are in operation, criteria dictated by the artist, the situation, and perhaps by the means of recording.

We often focus on the wrong things in Mik's videos; but curiously what we fail to find there corresponds to common techniques of filmmaking, to particular camera shots and editing principles. There are no interactions between individuals, no actions and reactions (i.e., no shot/reverse shot). There is no individual expression (no close-up). There is no deviation of activity (no change of shot). And finally, there is no intervening event or crisis, no development, climax, or resolution (no editing).

In spite of the unvarying camera shots and lack of editing we sense a complicity between shot and action even if the recording sometimes has a detachment about it. In most of his recent videos, Mik uses one type of camera shot. In *Softer Catwalk in Collapsing Rooms*, *Organic Escalator*, *Lumber* (all 2000), *Glutinosity* and *Reversal Room* (both 2001), either a tracking shot slowly traverses the scene or a zoom shot penetrates the set. While continually adjusting the framing of the scene, the shots parallel, complement or replicate the flow of the action, or integrate the viewer to it.

The tracking shot tends to distance us from the action in Mik's videos. We look on, unperturbed, passive or alienated. But so, sometimes, do the figures within. In *Softer Catwalk in Collapsing Rooms*, a tracking shot paces back and forth parallel to the collapsing set through which detached individuals trek almost as if they were sleepwalking from room to room. We sense the artificiality of the set at the same time as we are aware that we see it by means of a camera tracking at its edge. The zoom shot, on the contrary, tends to include us, but at the cost of unbalancing. The camera in *Organic Escalator*, for instance, moves shallowly in and out towards an escalator on which a huddled mass of beings individually twist and

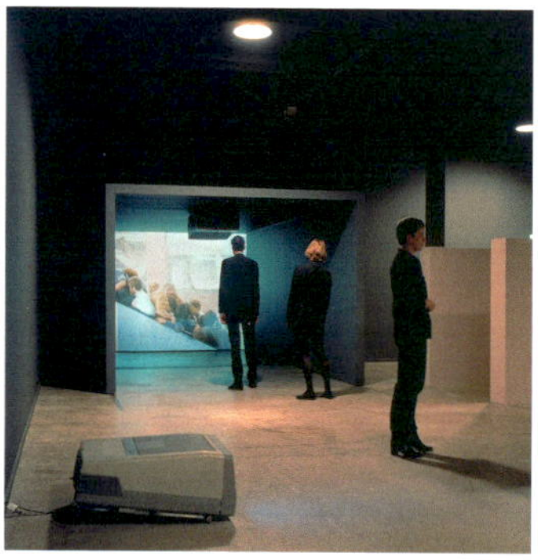

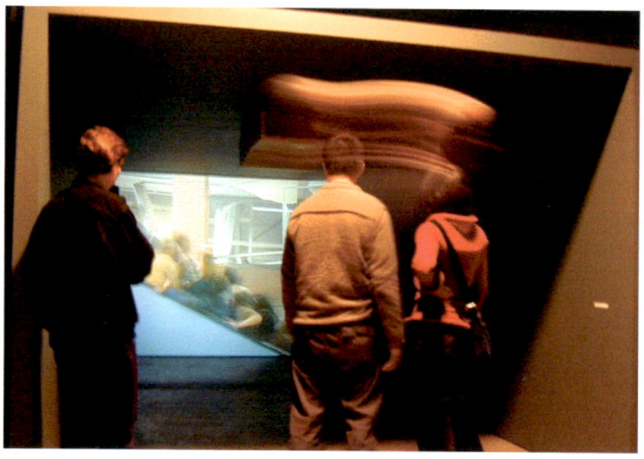

turn and slide as a group, up and down its steps. The zoom's rhythm is accented by the forward and backward swaying of the collapsing set. The lightweight construction dangles precariously, but the participants are under no threat. This is no disaster and there is no panic; the threat of injury is unnaturally absent. The set remakes itself and collapses again and again. While as viewers we are under no threat, even of mimetic identification, nonetheless we feel a disturbance. For simultaneously the whole room in which the image is housed (which contains us as well), moves forward and backward, the projector and screen in tandem with it. Nothing in the image is distorted, only our certainty of where the zoom is occurring — inside or outside the image. Of course, the truth is it is happening in both. Camera, action, and space join in an organic whole, as if a breathing entity.

Sometimes the two shots are combined, as in *Reversal Room* (to be discussed later), or seem to be, as in *Glutinosity*. In *Glutinosity*, the camera tracks across the narrowly confined space of a riot but also irregularly seesaws into the mêlée as if it was climbing over fallen bodies. Internal to the scene, individual actions mimic the types of shots: supine bodies shunt back and forth parallel to the tracking shot in and out of the frame, while others tilt forward and backward, perpendicular to the screen.

Our perception is guided by expectation. When expectations are not met, we are initially confused. In *Glutinosity*, the uncertainty of our perception is matched by our puzzlement at the action. A decomposing and recomposing struggle takes place between protesters and security in a scene we might recognize from tele-

Organic Escalator (installation views), 2000

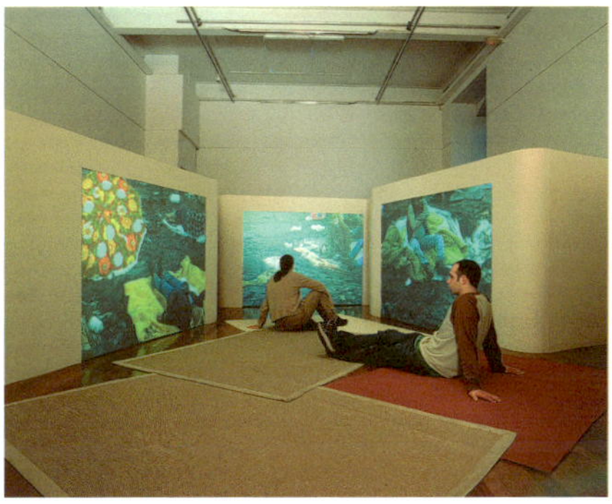

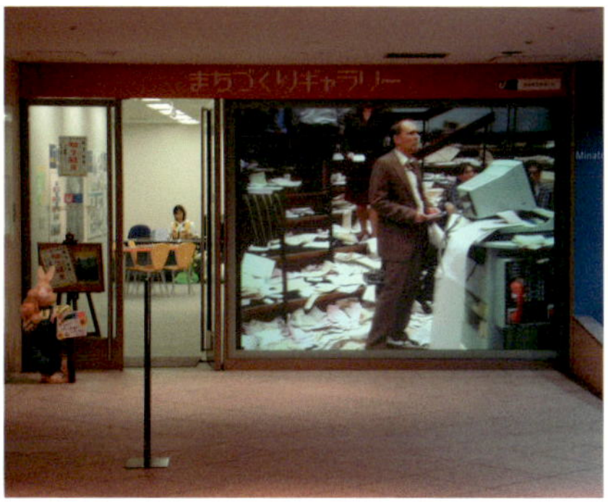

vision news reports as an anti-globalist protest. But here the stakes seem no more than a serpentine interplay acted out in the tightly foregrounded space of the back and forth tracking shot. The mock violence dissipates in a tumult of generality. Not only are details missing in this reconstruction: security lack any weapons, for instance. Aggression notably is absent between the contestants. Costumes code oppositional sides, but action seems determined by more abstract rules constructed by the scenic conditions of a film shoot.

This series of works marks a reversal in Mik's composition of actions. The early works start with unfamiliar activity which, over time, we come to accept, because of its persistence and lack of deviation, as quasi-normal. In *Suck* (1996), floating guitarists are prodded and pulled by industrial porto-vacs. In *Kitchen* (1997), three old men mock fight in faked slow motion. In more recent work, the scenes first present themselves as familiar but become stranger as we look at them. Indeed, most are scenes of a type we already know through the various disasters or disruptions conveyed to us by television news or entertainment — for instance, the protest mimicked in *Glutinosity*. But with no story line, their status is ambiguous. The appropriateness of our response is stayed. Is *Glutinosity* a riot or an elaborate play? Are the scenes of *Lumber* — five tracking shots of a mud-drenched field, occupied by grunge youth lying disheveled on blankets, plastic sheets, and air mattresses — the outcome of a rain-soaked pop festival or the aftermath of a disaster? Nothing tells us which. We cannot decide. There is no evidence the camera can witness. The unobtrusive, objective gaze of the camera records only entropic

Left: ***Lumber*** **(installation view)**, 2000 Right: ***Middlemen*** **(installation view)**, 2001

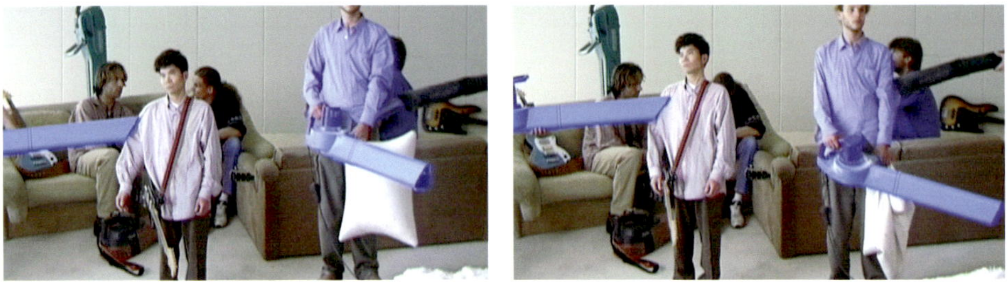

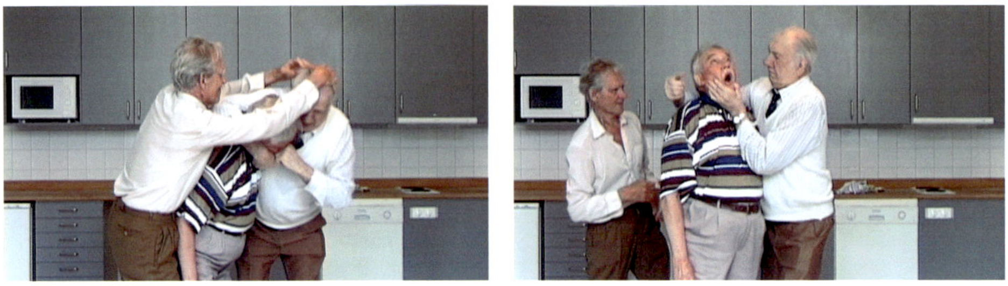

Top: ***Suck***, 1996
video installation

Bottom: ***Kitchen***, 1997
video installation

equivalencies: the viscous mud, the trampled blankets, the passive bodies. Only occasionally some of the reclining bodies heave unnaturally.

Mik has re-staged type of events we generally classify as crises. However if there were crises, they have already happened. In his videos, we always seem to enter in the middle of things, but even if we waited for the looping of the scenes, we would not return to any precipitating event. In that return, we are not even sure what we have already seen as there is no start or finish, only the continuum of an unending panorama. No more do we sense that something happened off-screen or previously. Rather, we come to accept that the activity in any particular Mik work is part of a closed system, operating according to its own dynamics and laws.

States of crises persist as much as any other routine action, but without fluctuation or resolution. *Middlemen* (2001), with its litter-strewn floor, seems the aftermath of some stock market meltdown. Some brokers sit exhausted, some run through the space, while others take notes, appearing to watch a big board off-screen. Yet nothing happens; no computers are on, no telephones are used; no one trades or communicates. The camera meanders through the space, back and forth, in and out with no particular rhythm, focus or logic. Sometimes it suddenly zooms coincident with a bodily jerk from someone in view. A wave of spasms and tics is the only suggestion that a shock might be dissipating through the crowd. Yet, we notice one lethargic body, a dopplegänger of the man sitting beside him, wearing the same company plaid blazer. He has the same features and mimics the motion of his partner, except with a swaying roll to his body; as it turns out he is a puppet about fifteen per cent larger. Of course, he can have no intentionality to his actions and his presence begs the question: Can the others in Mik's videos, then, be agents of theirs?

Is this puppet finally emblematic of Mik's deterministic world where the artist sets all the rules? The constant we observe in all his work is that routine is the rule — routine as a continuity of action, stripped of intention, rationale, and end. No event sets the actions in motion; they persist at one level of intensity, even if they appear to be the aftermath of a crisis. Ultimately, though, we cannot even say what has taken place. The actions just are; they have no event status to them. It is exactly the languages of action and event we have to dispense with in considering Mik's work. We have to find another language to describe what takes place in spite of the fact that the artist may build our preconceived expectations into his installations. Entering his installations, we must temporarily surrender our own agency in order to see what happens.

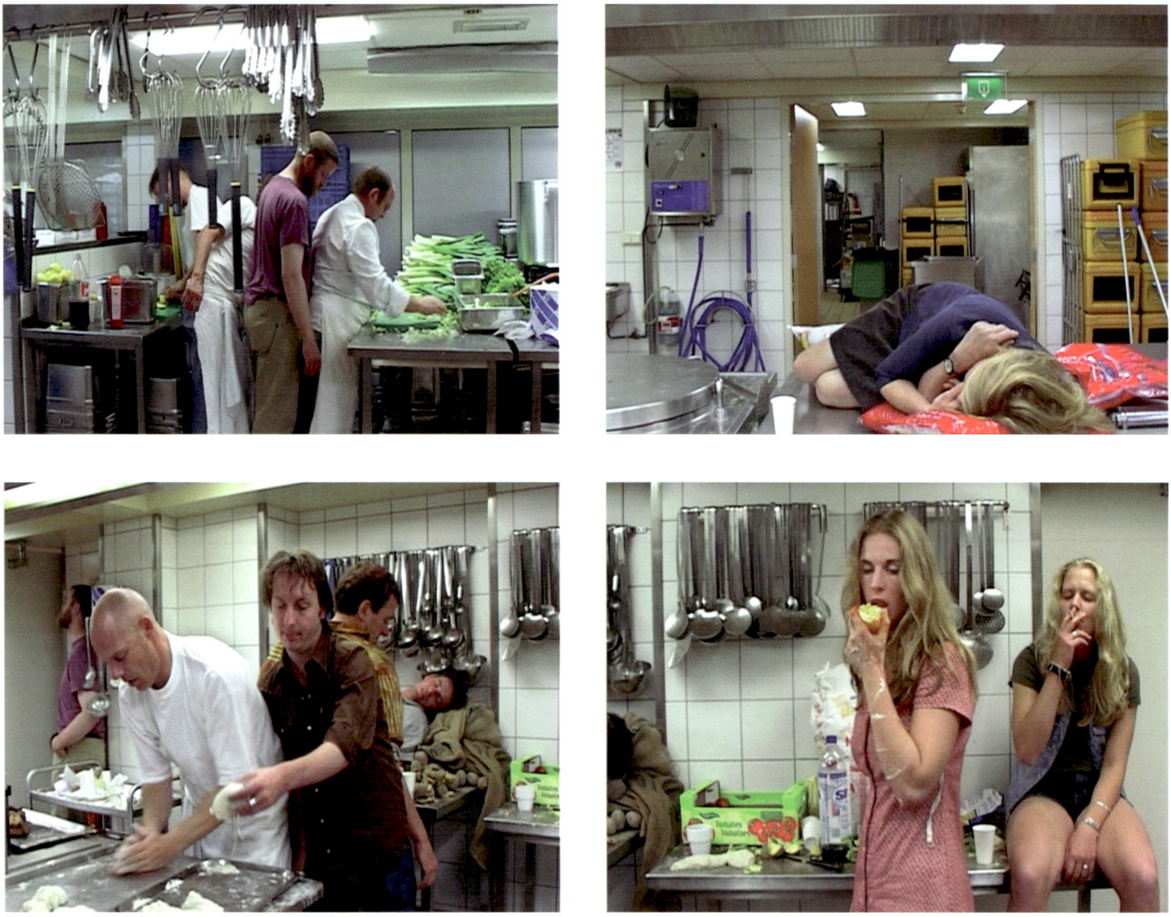

Reversal Room, 2001

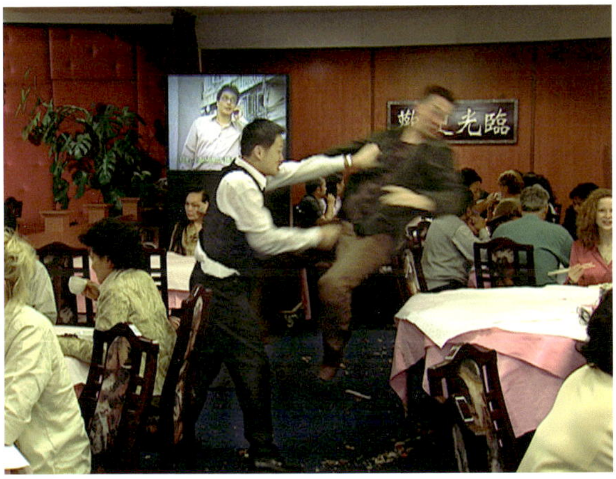

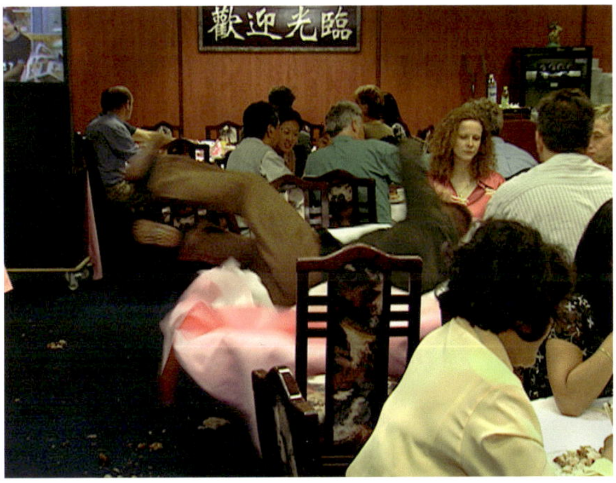
歡迎光臨

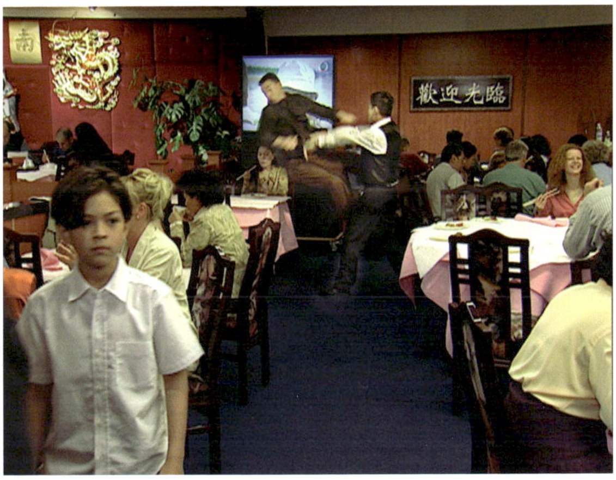
南
歡迎光臨

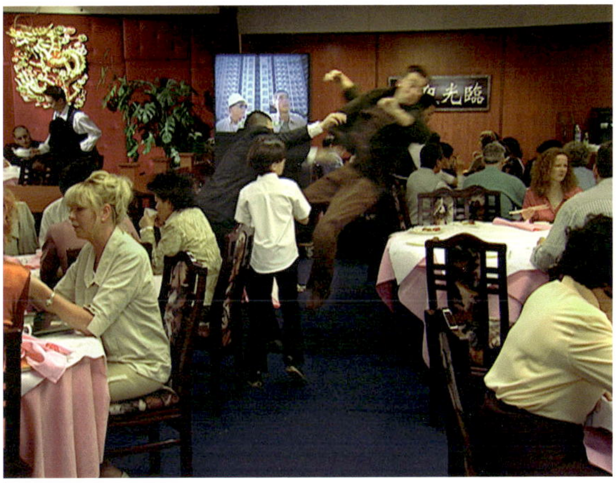

Quasi-Events, Void Intentions, Neuter Actions

In Mik's *Reversal Room*, everything proceeds in doubles. This doubling is not mirror-like; it always produces two separate but parallel realms. These realms might be contiguous or continuous to one another; yet somehow at some point they intersect. It is up to us to decide whether this intersection qualifies as an event or whether we have to think about it in other terms that the whole structure puts into play. For everything in *Reversal Room* is a construction — from its doubled scene to its double seeing.

We have already tacitly accepted the conventions that Mik's work puts into place — first, its gallery setting, second, the architectural housing for the rear-projection video images that leads us into and contains us within its space. (The specially constructed enclosure, which houses the screens, encircles the spectator with a two-meter high wall with a wide entrance and a narrow exit.) We take the images to be primary: they are what we are here to view. Furthermore, we expect what happens within them to conform to either one of two standards: to what we know of behaviour "out there," or to what we experience of it through the moving images of film and television.

Everything in *Reversal Room* has been made to guide our attention. Within that fabrication, we are drawn naturally to what attracts our look, to what moves; it is a *video* installation, after all. We substitute what we see there for our own activity — other people's behaviour for our own — and so we come to a halt before these moving images.

The action in Mik's videos, however, resembles nothing we are familiar with and immediately throws us. The behaviour is off somehow, but we can't seem to place what exactly is wrong about it, partly because the activity seems to impart itself as — almost — normal. *Reversal Room* is no different than any other Mik installation in this regard, except that for the first time in his work we are presented with two separate scenes of activity. (Like *Lumber*, *Reversal Room* was shot with five cameras and displayed on five screens.) In each of these scenes, two streams of activity take place.

One scene takes place in a Chinese restaurant and the other in a kitchen that obviously is unrelated to the restaurant. In the restaurant, two male white patrons separately leave their table, appearing to seek out the Asian owner or a waiter amongst the crowded tables and accost them, only to be manhandled and thrown on top of either one of two occupied dining tables. The patrons recover, dust themselves off, retreat to their table, only to re-enact their slapstick routine again and again. The other diners pay no attention, not even those inconvenienced by the table collapsing, and the table pops back up by itself and is reset as the dinner resumes. In the kitchen, two groups — uniformed chefs and kitchen help who belong there, and casually dressed guests who are trespassing — occupy the same tight space but exist almost in different temporal zones. While the staff bustles, preparing food, the guests dawdle, creating a mess. Each is oblivious to the other, even though the guests sometimes shadow the staff around the room. While staff and guests exist in the same space, their temporal worlds do not seem to intersect.

An element uncommon to each scene interferes, something unfamiliar, unconventional or unnatural to the context: the fights of the restaurant scene, the guests in the kitchen. The intrusive presence of both is not inconceivable. Fights can spontaneously erupt anywhere; a private party could spill into and mill about a restaurant kitchen. Yet, in each we have the sense that certain modes of conduct are normal or appropriate to the context, others not. The behaviour of the fighters and guests is not only inappropriate, it is also abnormal. For instance, the anger expressed by the restaurant agitators does not follow a typical fight curve. It is already dissipated from the start as if something was missing from their psychology. But, then, the behaviour of the other diners is not normal either. Their indifference is peculiar. So perhaps is the discipline of the cooks who tolerate the nonchalance of their guests. Collectively they go about their routine tasks, as inconclusive as they seem in light of the fact that nothing actually gets made. We wonder, however, why the guests behave as members of a group, even as they are distinct from one another. Each guest mimics her or his companions in some unproductive labour, reversing that of the cooks.

The actions of the two groups in the kitchen parallel one another without interaction. The participants seem to move to different tempos. No eye contact is made, no gestures are shared, there is no give or take of recognition or communication. (Both video sequences are silent. In the restaurant, the patrons can be seen to converse; in the kitchen, all are mute.) It is as if we see a double exposure of the same space at different times with two sets of inhabitants, or as if we witness a ghost world intervening with the real world. Yet the two groups in the kitchen link together when the guests tail the workers around the space or hunch over them while they work. The contrast of their body language — one industrious, the other lethargic — does not necessarily suggest opposition so much as co-existence on a scale of activity that ranges from the dynamic to the static. Or perhaps the two activities register different phases of entropy. To every productive action of the cooks — chopping leeks, slicing lemons or potatoes, frying chops — we can pose an unproductive, "destructive," near-unconscious play by the guests: pulling food apart, pushing or dumping it on the floor, even sleeping on piles of potatoes.

If the activities in the kitchen parallel one another as if in a distorting mirror, in the restaurant they interpenetrate — the fighting disrupts the tranquil scene. Yet, if we observe closely, the fighters and diners do not really intermingle. Aside from the temporarily inconvenient collapsing tables, the unfazed diners pay no heed; their conversations proceed unabated. The fighters' interruption leaves no turbulence in its wake; no waves of agitation ripple through the dining room and then settle. In what respect and in what reality do the two groups intersect? As they seem to have no effect on one another, are they two streams of activity with different wavelengths? (We note that the absence or exhaustion of motivation in the actions of the restaurant agitators is complementary, not contrary, to the obliviousness of the other diners.) On a different scale of measure, or if we were patient enough to witness long waves of a continuum, the interruption may not seem disruptive. Repetition and continuity would coalesce. One would not become the event of the other. Why should we concentrate on the intrusion of the fight as if the context of dining is merely a background for this event? The periodic repetition of the fights and the continuity of indifference of the diners are two planes of activity that intersect in another dimension, which means that the irruption of the fight is no more an event than the continuity of dining is a non-event.

If norms of response are absent, those corresponding to the determinations of will and milieu, other "laws" dictating the action of the body are in operation in this universe. In Mik's works behaviour is influenced by abstract relations such as space and time, with one regulating activity more than the other. For instance, the intrusions depicted in *Reversal Room*'s two scenes differ in nature: the kitchen guests' interruption is spatial, while the restaurant fighters' is temporal.

Nonplussed by both the lack of intention and the indirection of activity, we still stubbornly seek relationships. Since *Reversal Room* shows two scenes, we naturally look for a connection between them, not only a comparison and contrast of their types of behaviour, but some sort of narrative link between individual stories. Mik frustrates our demand for narrative; there is no association between the two scenes (the kitchen does not provide the back story to the restaurant and no characters pass between them), nor are there individual stories or character development within them. However, there is a minor overlapping between the two scenes in that the mimicry of the kitchen is repeated in the restaurant as an Asian boy follows the owner around the restaurant.

Mik doesn't assist us by means of any typical narrative guides. He doesn't conceive of the sequences as having a beginning, middle, or end; he loops long takes. As well, he chooses not to edit, and in so doing refuses the use of montage to manipulate our look and to tell a story following the traditional dramatic pattern of accelerating action, climax, and denouement. The fights, for instance, do not follow a similar dynamic.

The cameras repeat this indifference, neglecting to focus on anything that might qualify as an event. However the cameras' indifference does not mean that they have no effect — that they are transparently recording the activities. Mik's construction of the shot dictates the action in the same manner that his construction of the installation controls our manner of movement and looking within it. Action, camera movement and spatial construction link up in an apparatus that implicates us.

I have neglected to say what the main "event" of the installation is. *Reversal Room* exists in two parts, but we do not move through one to the other. Rather unusually, the two parts of the work displace each other successively — i.e., temporally — within the same space. Suddenly the installation changes. Mik has engineered it so that the same five rear-projection screens will display two sets of five synched images successively. Simultaneous with the switch on the five screens, the colour of the lighting changes from warm to cool, or vice versa, and two small rooms either come into view or are hidden by one-way mirrors. Of the same height as the surrounding walls, the two rooms are inaccessible, although we notice a back door ajar in one and a side table of the same manufacture as the two in our space in the other. As one scene changes to another, the mirror image of furniture materializes into an actual object.

Both video sequences are shot with five cameras simultaneously, but a different type of camera shot is used exclusively in each. In the restaurant scene, the cameras slowly zoom in and out, all directed from different angles toward roughly one area of the room, with each image expanding and contracting at different ratios. In the kitchen scene, a 360-degree pan shot rotates slowly across all five screens, the five cameras together circumscribing the whole room. Within the image, the movement of actors corresponds to the camera shot. In the restaurant, we see them zigzagging through the space, converging towards the cameras in different perspectives. In the kitchen, the stationary actors slowly slide by or they make quick circuits around the room passing from screen to screen.

The two types of shots are reflected in the architecture of the installation itself: the enclosure is round when its mirrors hide the rooms during the kitchen panorama; then it becomes star-shaped when these rooms are revealed, reflecting the depth of the restaurant zooms. As viewers we perceptually replay these camera movements in the space. Sometimes we see ourselves reflected as virtual images adjacent to the panoramic projections; at other times our eyes penetrate the real spaces opened up analogous to the virtual spaces of the zoom images. Flush to the ground, the rear-projection screens mask the division between the virtual space of the image and the actual space of our participation. The scale of the figures within the images, proportional to our own in their spatial perspective, contributes to this sense of passage between the two zones.

Usually Mik emphasizes this continuity by maintaining ambient lighting in the space to naturalize or detheatricalize the adjacency of actual and virtual zones, so different from what we experience seated in movie houses. He strives to keep our situation at ease. However, in *Reversal Room* he unsettles us. The work's reversals perpetually put us in contradictory states. Actual and virtual flip back and forth. "Accessible" and "forbidden" keep revising their terms. Already ambiguous, what seems visually or physically penetrative changes from switch to switch. Psychologically, we can "walk" into the image — just as the mirrors virtually project us into the small rooms — whereas we know we cannot walk through the glass of the revealed rooms. The "transparency" of the screen confers a different status than the glass: we can see through the glass, but we know it physically halts us.

Mik takes some of the inherent oppositions or "reversals" of the body — for example, that we can see further than we can physically reach — and builds their structural conditions into the installation, complicating them by varying their circumstances in actual and virtual spaces. Do the two camera shots, panorama and zoom, similarly reflect the two functions of the eye, scanning and focusing? Moreover, do they register our participation opposingly, as passive and active respectively?

Adding movement to these virtualities, Mik introduces a temporal factor.

Activity takes place over time. The spatial and the temporal intersect according to different modalities, just as the actual and the virtual do. Our continuous feeling of being spatially unbalanced, amplified by the slight variations and wobbles of the camera movements, is temporally reinforced by the timing of the switch between the two scenes. Since the twenty-minute long sequences are programmed to switch randomly at any time between ten to twenty minutes, we can never predict when the change will happen — we are always surprised.

Before the switch between the two scenes, I paid attention to what happened within the frame, not because of it. After the startle of the switch, I looked for what was common between the two scenes and determined that the behaviour, whether parallel or interpenetrative, functioned on scales of active/indifferent and static/dynamic. Because I paid no heed to the overall framework in which my experience was embedded, I was still inattentive. We need to look for these scalar relationships not only in the actions themselves, but also within the constraints of the apparatus as a whole on our behaviour. We have to pay attention to what happens not just within the various frames (scene, shot, space), but also between the frames and because of them, recognizing that each inscribes at least a double space and a double time. The relationships we have to discover are those by which we participate in Mik's installation.

These relationships have nothing to do with the conventional expectations we had when we entered. These expectations are formed by a lifetime of observing behaviour, cinematic models, and the codes of language. It's naive to say that we have to abandon every convention we tacitly observed in entering *Reversal Room* and watching its images, be it the language of intentionality defining behaviour or the montage of shots in films. My writing can do nothing to dispel them. For instance, my summaries of the two scenes were composed of incidents that I found significant to relate. They ordered a narrative my language unconsciously reproduces, but they do not necessarily describe what "happens." The "what happens" or, more properly, the "happening" can only be experienced in the work because we are part of it.

The shooting and the activity of the scenes do not assume the same temporal form as my description. It is as if my description and Mik's video transcription, while having the same referents, also occupy different realms — like the protagonists of the mismatched kitchen worlds — and order experience differently. To bring them more into alignment, we would have to settle into another frame of consciousness.

In jostling two realities — within the scenes, between them, and between them and ourselves — *Reversal Room* exposes another reversal: between movement in the image and passivity in the viewer, the inaugural cinematic trope. It is not as if we are awakened by the switch to reverse these terms. In Mik's works we must always diffuse any event into a longer continuum of being, while recognizing, at the same time, our conflicted or mutually conditional active and passive roles within his constructions. While at any moment in *Reversal Room* we might be physically passive, we are still exposed to its durations. None of the events we witness or modes of experience we undergo has priority over any other; there is no hierarchy of judgement between so-called active and passive experiences. Variable, our experiences are always split within the temporal flow of life — whether within an artwork or not.

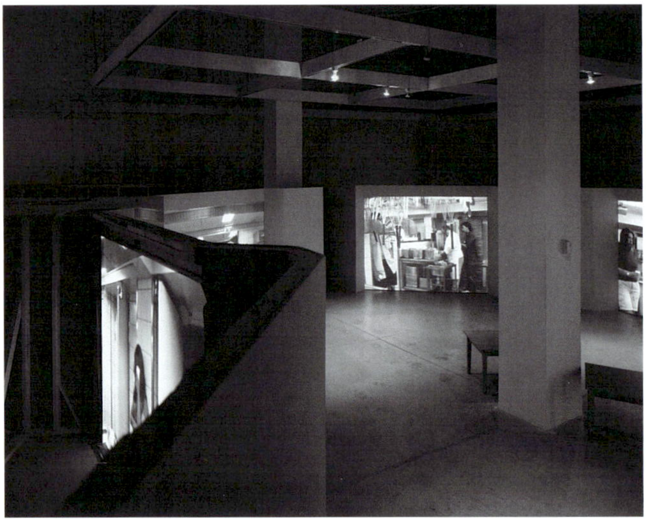
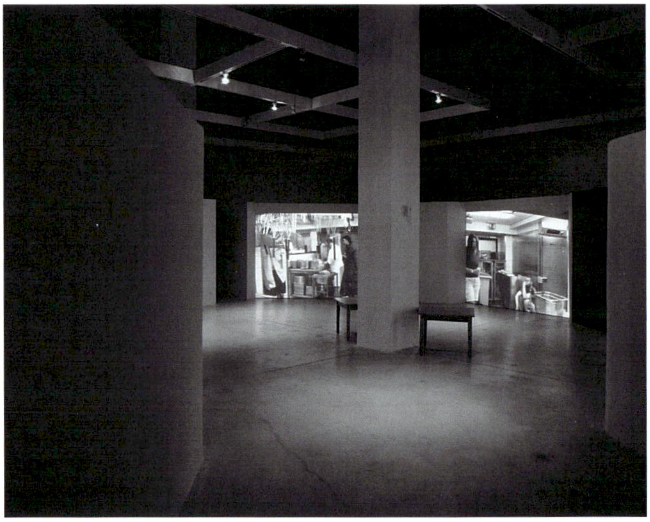
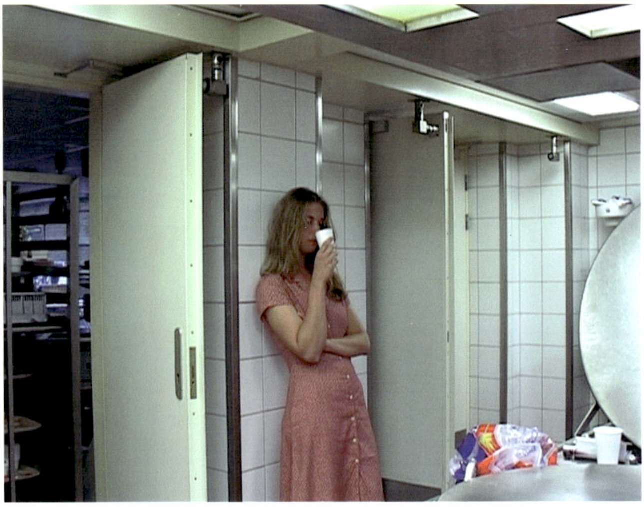
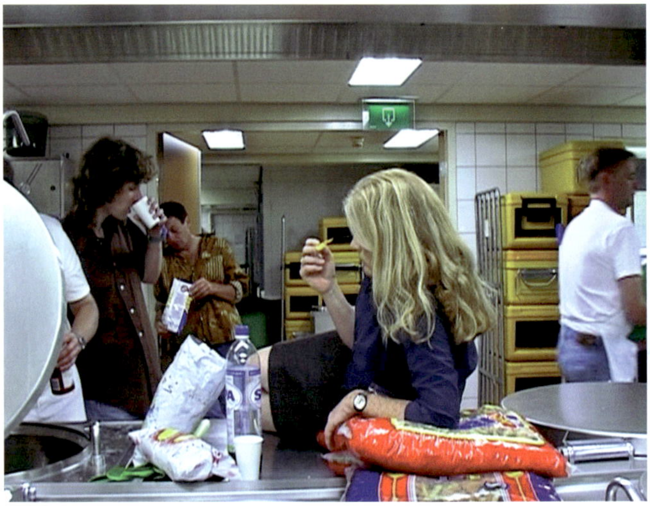

Top: *Reversal Room* (installation views), 2001

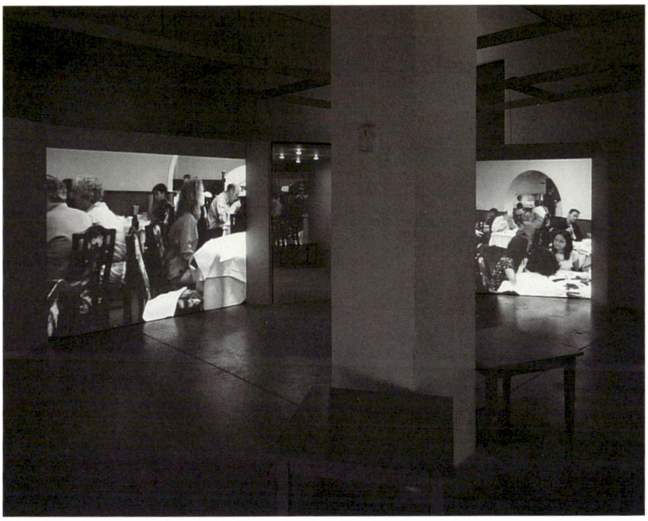

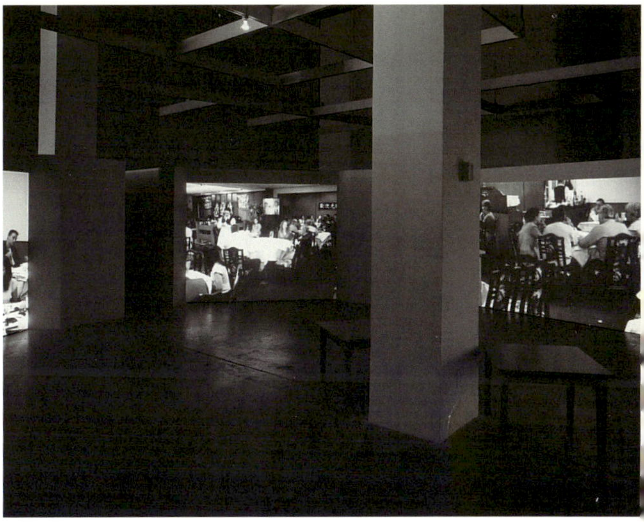

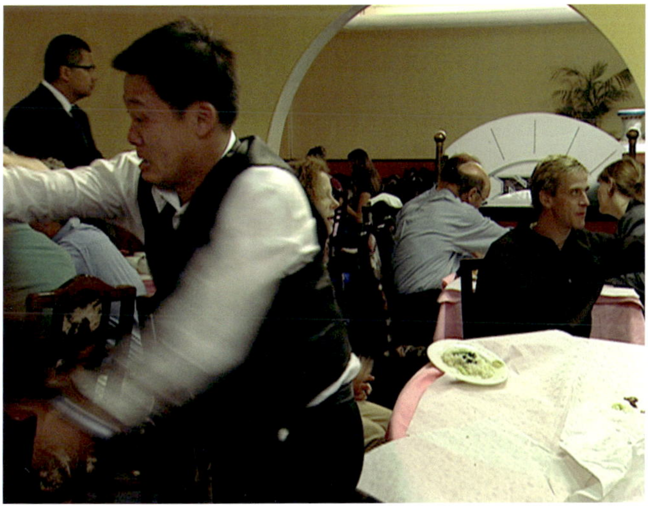

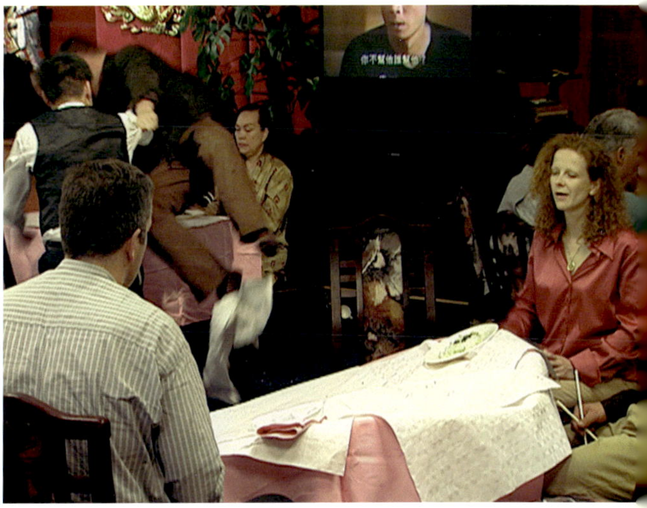

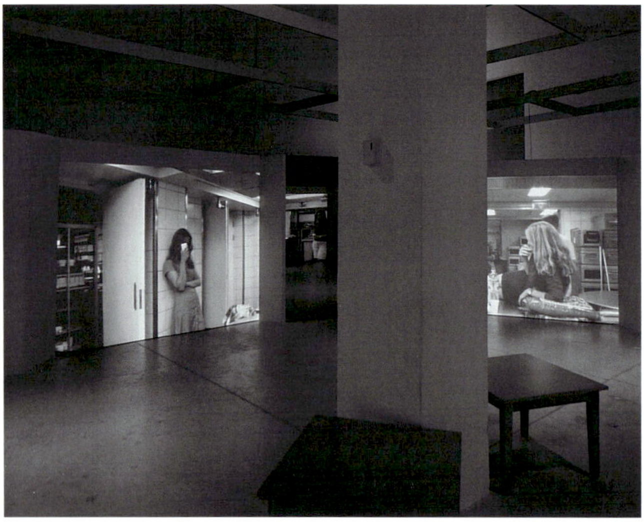

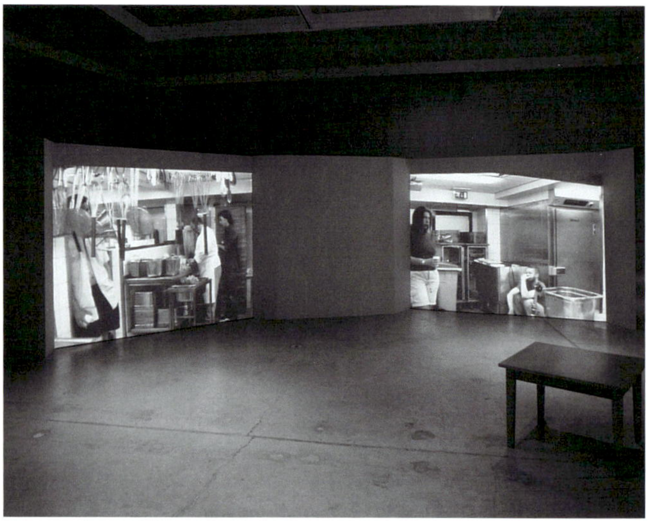

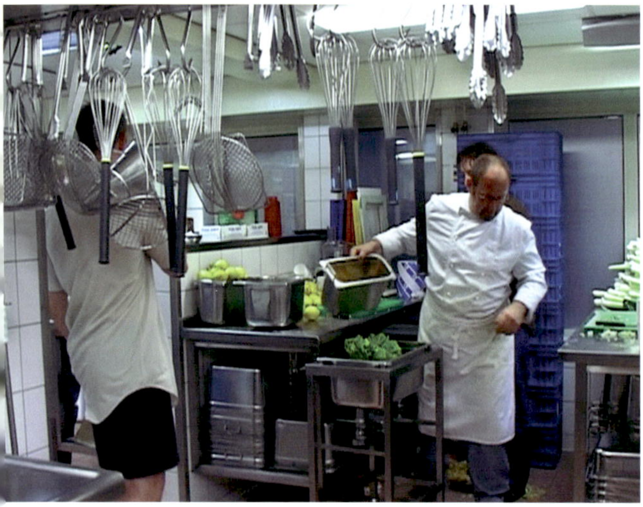

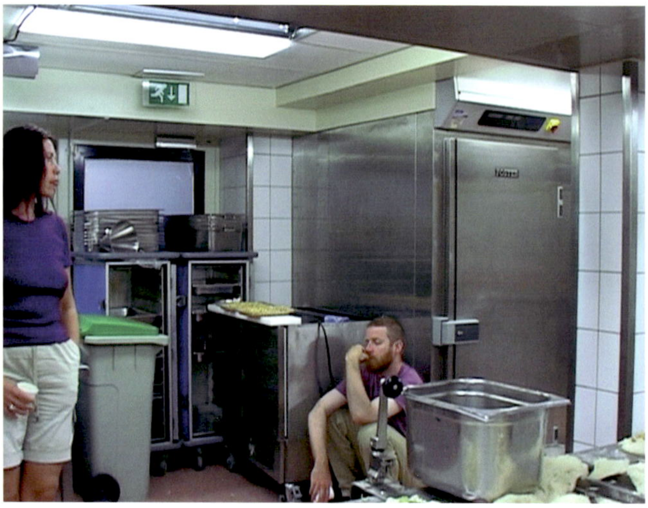

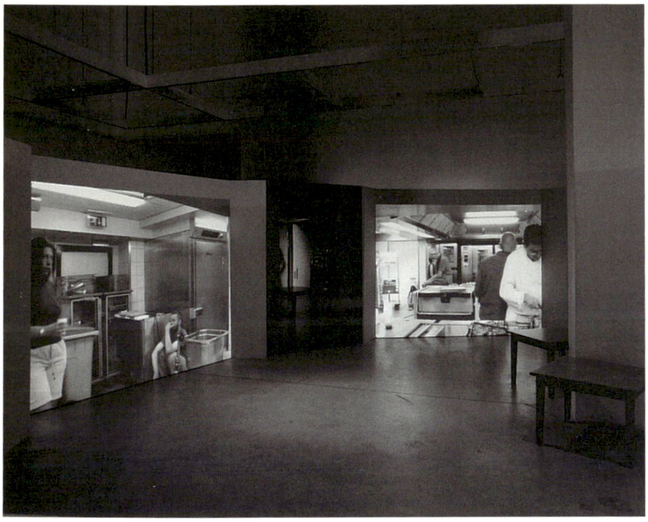

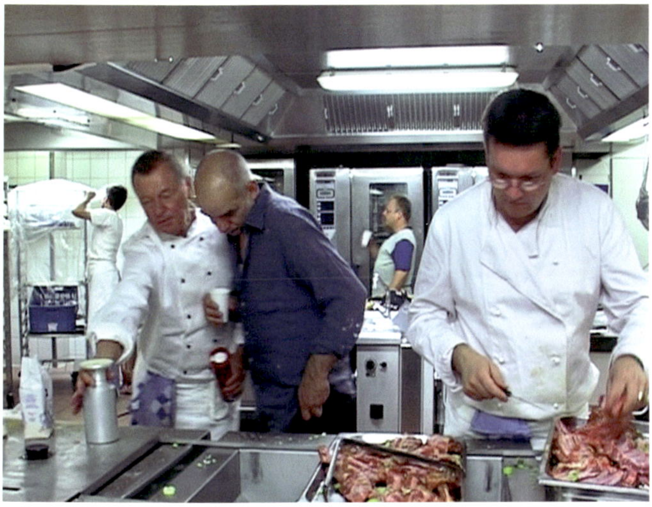

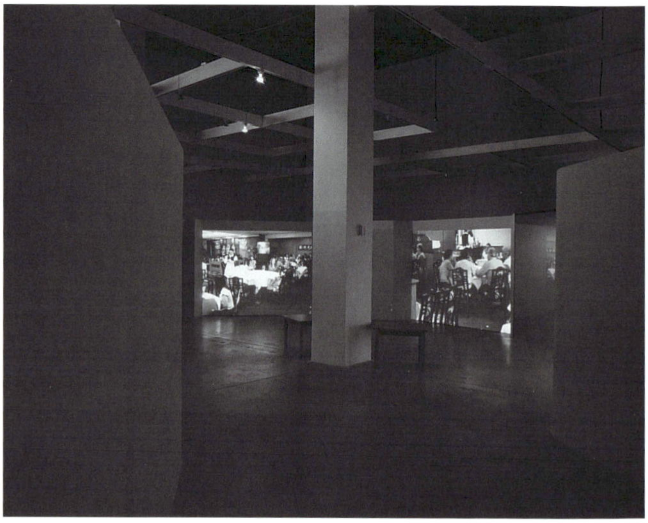

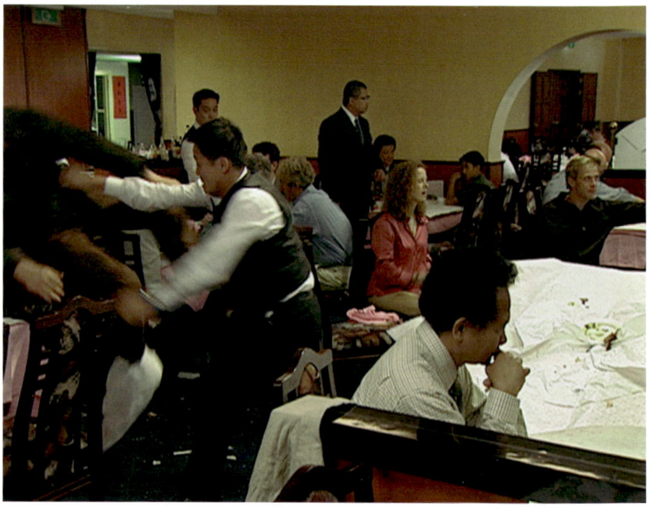

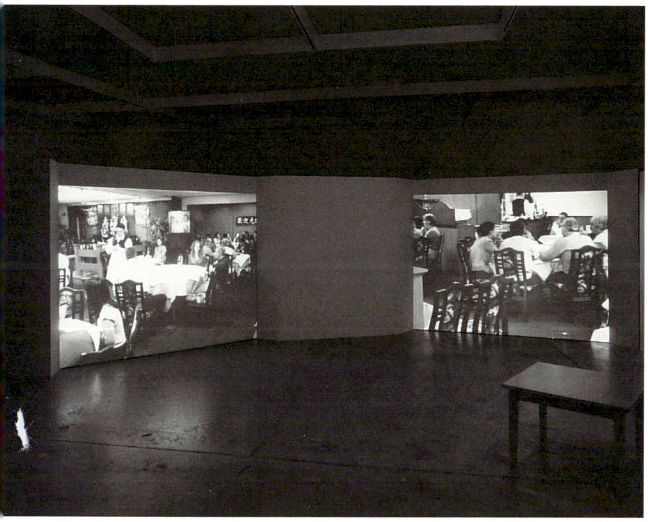

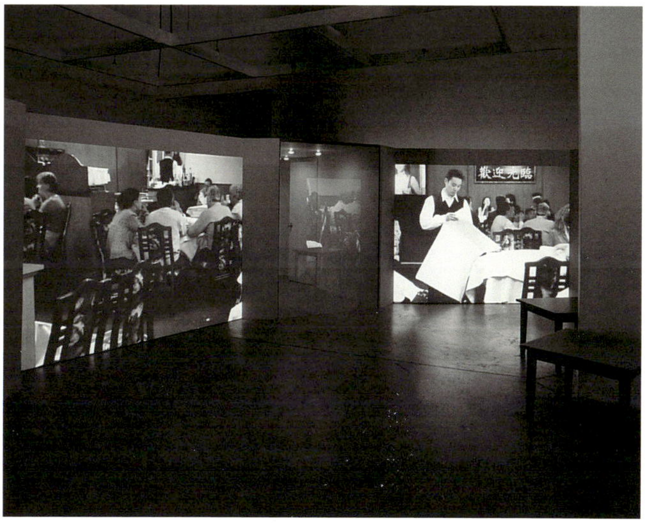
歡迎光臨

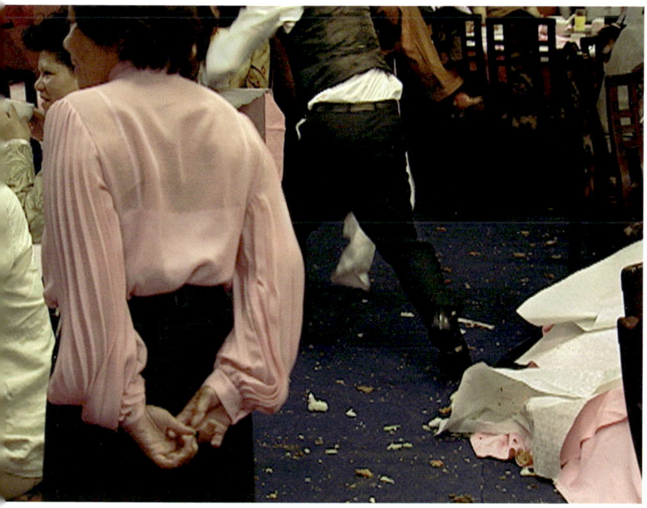

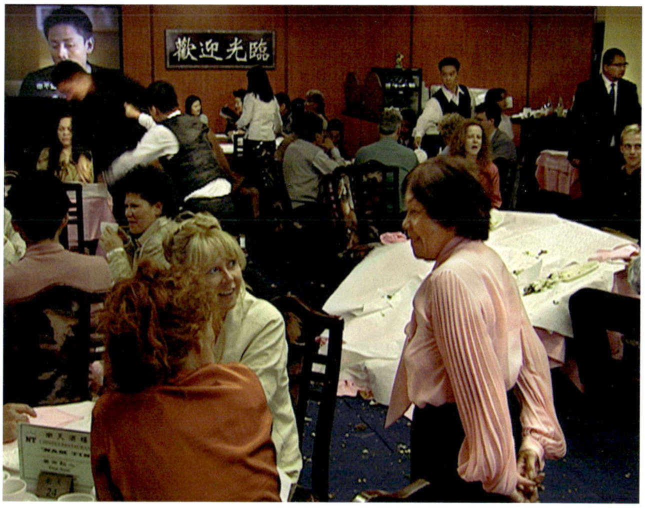
歡迎光臨

Image Credits

Reversal Room, 2001
digital video on DVD
5 screen video installation
edition of 4 + 1 a.p.
Camera: Benito Strangio
Directing Assistance: Marjoleine Boonstra
Special Effects: Robs Prop Shop
Production: Artfilm
Courtesy Carlier/Gebauer, Berlin

Middlemen, 2001
digital video on DVD
video installation
edition of 4 + 1 a.p.
Camera: Benito Strangio
Directing Assistance: Marjoleine Boonstra
Special Effects: Robs Prop Shop
Production: Artfilm
Courtesy Carlier/Gebauer, Berlin

Glutinosity, 2001
digital video on DVD
video installation
edition of 4 + 1 a.p.
Camera: Benito Strangio
Directing Assistance: Marjoleine Boonstra
Special Effects: Robs Prop Shop
Production: Artfilm
Courtesy Carlier/Gebauer, Berlin

Lumber, 2000
digital video on DVD
5 screen video installation
edition of 4 + 1 a.p.
Camera: Benito Strangio
Directing Assistance: Marjoleine Boonstra
Special Effects: Robs Prop Shop
Courtesy Carlier/Gebauer, Berlin

Organic Escalator, 2000
digital video on DVD
video installation
edition of 3 + 1 a.p.
Camera and Directing Assistance:
Marjoleine Boonstra
Special Effects: Robs Prop Shop
Courtesy Carlier/Gebauer, Berlin

Softer Catwalk in Collapsing Rooms, 1999
digital video on DVD
video installation
edition of 2 + 1 a.p.
Camera and Directing Assistance:
Marjoleine Boonstra
Special Effects: Robs Prop Shop
Courtesy Galerie Fons Welters, Amsterdam
and Carlier/Gebauer, Berlin

Biography and Bibliography

Aernout Mik
Born 1962, Groningen, the Netherlands
Lives and works in Amsterdam

Selected Solo Exhibitions

2002	*Aernout Mik: Reversal Room*, Stedelijk Museum Bureau Amsterdam, the Netherlands
	Flock, Fundacio Miro, Barcelona, Spain
2001	*Aernout Mik*, The Power Plant, Toronto, Canada
	Carlier/Gebauer, Berlin, Germany
2000	*Primal Gestures, Minor Roles*, Van Abbemuseum, Eindhoven, the Netherlands
	3 Crowds, Institute of Contemporary Arts, London, UK
1999	*Hanging Around*, Museum Ludwig, Cologne, Germany
1997	*XLVll Venice Biennale*, Dutch Pavillion, Italy
1995	*Wie die Räume gefüllt werden müssen*, Kunstverein, Hannover, Germany

Selected Group Exhibitions

2002	*Tableaux Vivants*, Kunsthalle Wien, Austria
2001	*Yokohama Triennale*, Yokohama, Japan
	Berlin Biennale, Berlin, Germany
1999	*Signs of Life*, Melbourne Biennial, Melbourne, Australia
	In All the Wrong Places, Ottawa Art Gallery, Ottawa, Canada
1998	*Hongkongoria* (with Marjoleine Boonstra), Van Abbemuseum, Eindhoven, the Netherlands
1996	*The Scream*, Arken Museum of Modern Art, Copenhagen, Denmark
	ID, Van Abbemuseum, Eindhoven, the Netherlands
1995	*Wild Walls*, Stedelijk Museum, Amsterdam, the Netherlands

Selected Publications

Kopsa, Maxine, Mark Kremer, Tijs Goldschmidt and Bernhard Balkenhol. *Primal Gestures, Minor Roles.* Eindhoven: Van Abbemuseum, 2000.

Monk, Philip. *Aernout Mik: Reversal Room.* Toronto: The Power Plant, 2002.

Monk, Philip. *Reversal Room.* Amsterdam: Stedelijk Museum Bureau, 2002.

Walsh, Anne and Martijn van Nieuwenhuyzen. *3 Crowds.* London: Institute of Contemporary Arts, 2000.

Walsh, Anne. *Tender Habitat.* Ann Arbor: The University of Michigan, 2000.

Acknowledgments

The Power Plant Contemporary Art Gallery at Harbourfront Centre is a registered Canadian charitable organization supported by Harbourfront Centre, the membership of The Power Plant, private donations, the City of Toronto through the Toronto Arts Council, the Ontario Arts Council and The Canada Council for the Arts.

The Power Plant Staff

Director
Wayne Baerwaldt

Assistant Director
Anette Larsson

Curator
Philip Monk

Head of Public Programmes, Education and Publicity
Kim Fullerton

Head of Membership
Katarina Berin

Interim Head of Membership
Kirsten Kamper

Head of Installation and Facilities
Paul Zingrone

Assistant Curator
Xandra Eden

Exhibition Coordinator
Laurel MacMillan

Membership Assistant
Antranik Tchalekian

Administrative Assistant
Francesco Corsaro

Corporate Relations Assistant
Rebecca Gimmi

Gallery Assistant
Angela Kotinkaduwa

Gallery Supervisor and Youth Programming Coordinator
Terence Dick

Animateurs
Gillian Atkins
Belinda Chun
Robert Durocher
Dave Kemp
Natasha Lan
Carson McKee
Alex Snukal

Exhibition Installation Crew
Neil Burns
Corinne Carlson
Sheila Dietrich
Julie Faris
Eric Glavin
Anitra Hamilton
Brad Johnson
Sean McQuay
Doug Moore
Mark Phillips
Chris Rogers

Publicity
Shari Lynn Sare

Website
Jill Murray

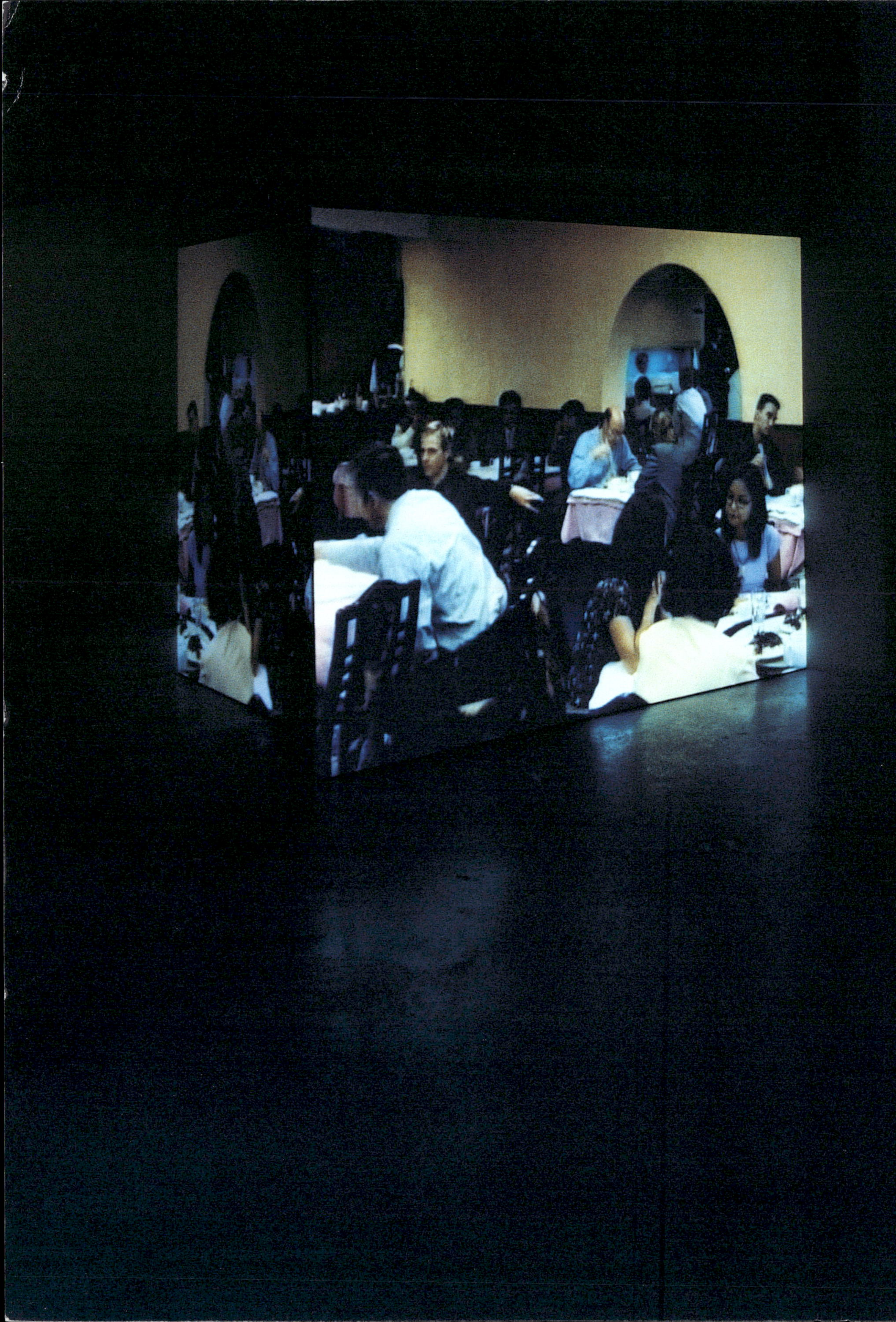

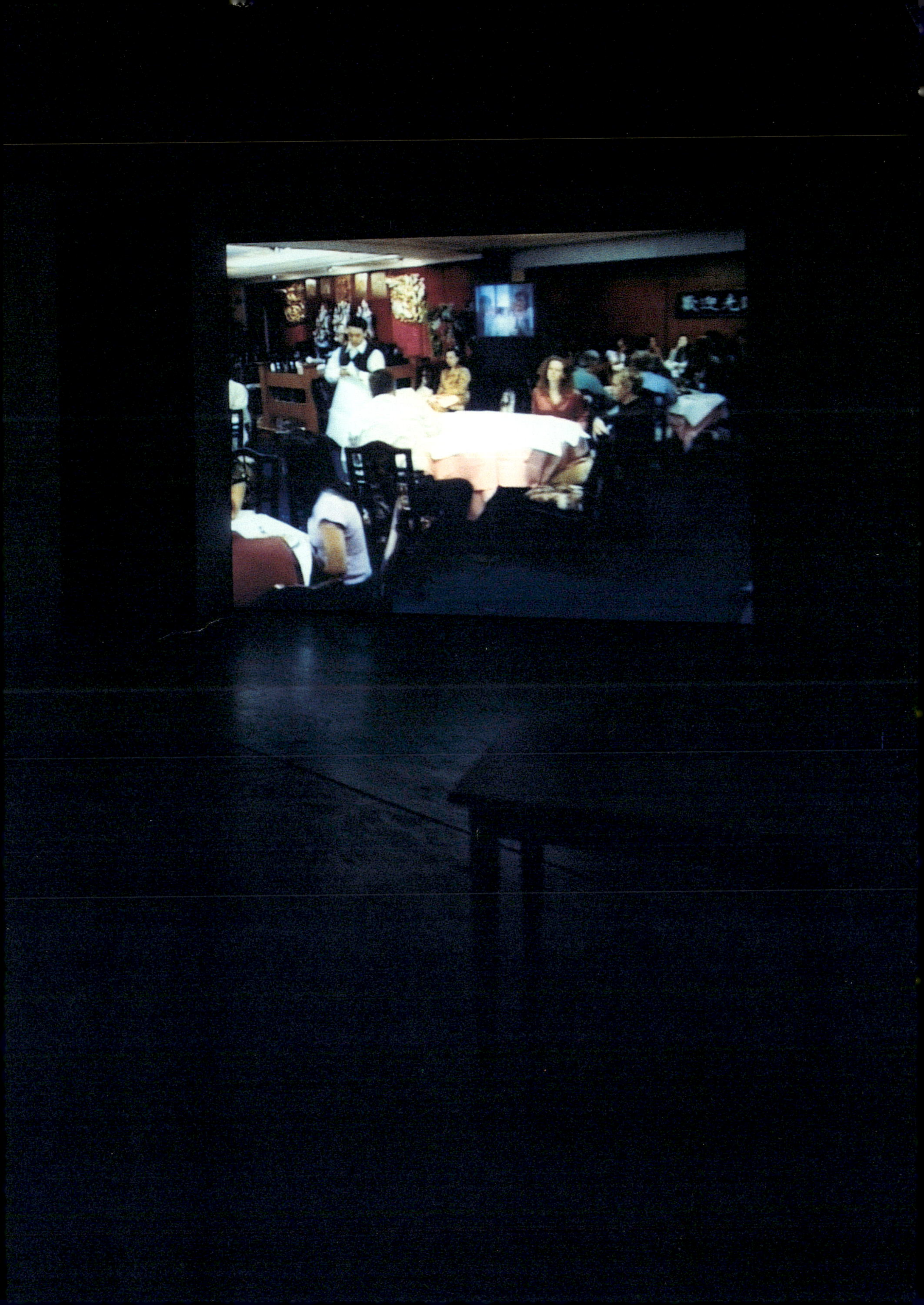

Catalogue Acknowledgments

Edited by Lisa Gabrielle Mark

Designed by Lewis Nicholson

Typeset by Richard Hunt at Archetype, Toronto

Printed in Canada by CJ Graphics Inc., Toronto

Photography:

pp. 2–3, 42–45, 50–51, ***Reversal Room,*** installation views at The Power Plant, 2001, Photos: Cheryl O'Brien.

p. 28, ***Organic Escalator***, installation views, Photos: Peter Cox.

p. 29, ***Middlemen,*** installation view at Yokohama Triennale, 2001.

Lumber, installation view at ICA, London, 2000.

Canada Council for the Arts Conseil des Arts du Canada

ONTARIO ARTS COUNCIL
CONSEIL DES ARTS DE L'ONTARIO

torontoartscouncil
An arm's length body of the City of Toronto